Do Yo

Your children's mo...
school is that their p...
the teacher and avoi~~d embarrassment?~~

Even the seemingly best teachers are easily tricked, and willingly trick themselves, into thinking that true education is going on?

The "mumbler," the "daydreamer," the "answer-grabber," the "eager failure," are just a few of the typical students who have evolved successful and ultimately destructive ways of getting through the school day.

From a young teacher's years of personal classroom experience and observation working with supposedly "bright" students in "above-average" schools has come a telling diagnosis of the mind-crippling malaise of current educational methods—and an urgent prescription for cure.

HOW CHILDREN
FAIL

John Holt

HOW CHILDREN FAIL

Introduction by
Allan Fromme, Ph.D.

A DELL BOOK

Published by
DELL PUBLISHING CO., INC.
750 Third Avenue
New York, N.Y. 10017

First Dell printing—January 1970
Second Dell printing—March 1970
Third Dell printing—May 1970
Fourth Dell printing—July 1970
Fifth Dell printing—October 1970
Sixth Dell printing—November 1970
Seventh Dell printing—February 1971

Acknowledgments

Like everyone else, I owe more debts than I can ever repay, or even tell. But to certain people, who have played a particularly important part in the development of this book and the ideas in it, I owe, and give, my special thanks: first, to Robert Cunningham, my English teacher at Exeter, who used to tell us, "Certainty is illusion, and repose is not the destiny of man," and thus, and for the first time, opened my mind to the possibility of doubt and change; then, to John and Anne Holden, directors of the Colorado Rocky Mountain School, and to Mary Wright, headmistress of the Lesley-Ellis School, who gave me classes to teach and left me free to teach them as I thought best, free to make mistakes and to learn what I could from them; to Peggy Hughes, who long urged and finally persuaded me to make these memos into a book; to my sister, Jane Pitcher, from whom I have learned a great deal about little children, and how to live with and enjoy them; to Bill Hull, who, more than anyone, made me look at, see, and think about what was really going on in the classroom and in the minds of the children I was trying to "teach"; finally, and most of all, to the children themselves, who taught me much more than I taught them.

Two Views on Education

"The purpose of a liberal arts education is to expand to the limit the individual's capacity, and desire, for self-education, for seeking and finding meaning, truth, and enjoyment in everything he does."

—A. WHITNEY GRISWOLD

"Why does a teaching machine insure thorough understanding?

Because the subject is broken down into small units that are easy for the student to handle and because questions are asked in a way that insures that the student gets the right answers almost all the time.

What is the 'right answer' habit?

A sense of accomplishment and confidence that the student acquires by moving successfully (getting right answers) through a programmed course of study at his own rate."

—FROM THE PROSPECTUS OF THE HONOR TEACHING MACHINE

"If we taught children to speak, they'd never learn."
—WILLIAM HULL

"Think things, not words."
—O. W. HOLMES, JR.

Introduction

Civilized life places us in a great variety of relationships with people. We buy from some and sell to others; play with some, fight with others. We know people as friends, relatives, policemen. One person is our doctor, another an uncle, a teacher, wife, father, daughter. Some of these relationships are formal, structured, definitive; others are loose, ill-defined, spontaneous. Some are superficial and thin, others involve our deepest feelings.

Contemporary psychological thought has come to stress the importance of exploring and understanding these relationships. The basic quality of our emotional maturity, we now realize, is largely the result of the events shaping the history of one of these relationships: that between parent and child. Defined almost as a testing ground for our personal adjustment, the marital relationship has become another major area of study.

Another relationship of great importance to the growth of the individual—and of even greater importance to the good of society—still cries out for study but remains generally neglected. Despite the fact that millions of children and thousands of adults are daily pressed into a student-teacher

relationship, we know very little about their inter-
actions and the influences they have on each other.
Of course, there is a great deal of material available on learning theory and general educational
practice, but none of this tells us what actually
happens when a teacher asks a child a question in
the classroom.

What *does* the child hear when he is called on?
What does he feel? What does he think? What are
his fantasies and wishes? What does he try to do?
What kinds of habits is he developing? What effect
does he have on the teacher? What does the
teacher think and feel and do as he awaits the
answer? Does he understand the meaning of the
child's answer or see it merely as right or wrong?
Does his relationship with the child have the
intimacy ideally necessary for intellectual growth
or is it a dull, contractual one which fosters *non-*
learning as much as it does learning?

Naturally, we cannot expect teachers all to be
clinical psychologists. But neither do we expect
husbands, wives, or parents to have doctoral de-
grees in marriage and family life. We expect them
to be sensitive human beings who will make an
effort to perceive many things in their relationship
for the purpose of getting the most out of it.
Teachers can be no more successful in the classroom than they can be in their marriages without
this quality of sensitivity. The reason for this is
that there is as much *intellectual* intimacy in the
teaching-learning relationship as there is *emotional*
intimacy in the husband-wife relationship.

Not every teacher is able or even willing to accept a relationship of such intimacy. Nor, for that
matter, is every student. It would be reasonable,

however, to expect the teacher to make a greater effort than the student does to promote interaction between them. But how? What can the teacher really do?

We cannot legislate sensitivity and intimacy into existence. We can define curriculum and theorize about motivation, but we cannot promote perception by command. Only by specific, concrete examples can we encourage teachers to learn *to see* their pupils, not their subject matter. Only by showing again and again what the *child* in the classroom is doing can we come to understand how he learns and how he fails to learn.

Failure in a success-oriented culture is hard to take. We are failing and our children are failing in our schools at an alarming rate. Even children who achieve enviable grades are failing to learn much of what we hope to teach them: abstraction, curiosity, and, most of all, appreciation. The subject matter of a course is frequently little more than merely a vehicle for the achievement of these educational goals—yet, all too often, the subject matter becomes an end in itself.

A teacher can perceive this only if he gets inside the mind of his pupil. John Holt has the rare capacity to do this, and, fortunately for us, he loses none of its richness and vividness when telling us about his work. For him, everyday teaching is what it should be: a process of mutual discovery, interaction, and exploration of the self as well as of another person and a subject matter. It is intensely alive, aware, sensitive. Mr. Holt has given us a book which should be immensely helpful. It is not like the performance of a musical virtuoso to which we listen appreciatively without any expectation that we can play as well. Mr. Holt's virtuosity as a teacher is laid before us in terms of insights we all can use; we are stimulated to use them as rapidly as we glean them from each page of his text.

Allan Fromme, PH.D.

Foreword

Most children in school fail.

For a great many, this failure is avowed and absolute. Close to forty percent of those who begin high school, drop out before they finish. For college, the figure is one in three.

Many others fail in fact if not in name. They complete their schooling only because we have agreed to push them up through the grades and out of the schools, whether they know anything or not. There are many more such children than we think. If we "raise our standards" much higher, as some would have us do, we will find out very soon just how many there are. Our classrooms will bulge with kids who can't pass the test to get into the next class.

But there is a more important sense in which almost all children fail: Except for a handful, who may or may not be good students, they fail to develop more than a tiny part of the tremendous capacity for learning, understanding, and creating with which they were born and of which they made full use during the first two or three years of their lives.

Why do they fail?

They fail because they are afraid, bored, and confused.

They are afraid, above all else, of failing, of disappointing or displeasing the many anxious adults around them, whose limitless hopes and expectations for them hang over their heads like a cloud.

They are bored because the things they are given and told to do in school are so trivial, so dull, and make such limited and narrow demands on the wide spectrum of their intelligence, capabilities, and talents.

They are confused because most of the torrent of words that pours over them in school makes little or no sense. It often flatly contradicts other things they have been told, and hardly ever has any relation to what they really know—to the rough model of reality that they carry around in their minds.

How does this mass failure take place? What really goes on in the classroom? What are these children who fail doing? What goes on in their heads? Why don't they make use of more of their capacity?

This book is the rough and partial record of a search for answers to these questions. It began as a series of memos written in the evenings to my colleague and friend Bill Hull, whose fifth grade class I observed and taught in during the day. Later these memos were sent to other interested teachers and parents. A small number of these memos make up this book. They have not been much rewritten, but they have been edited and rearranged under four major topics: Strategy; Fear and Failure; Real Learning; and How Schools Fail. *Strategy* deals with the ways in which children try to meet, or dodge, the demands that adults make of them in school. *Fear and Failure* deals with the interaction in children of fear and failure, and the effect of this on strategy and learning. *Real Learning* deals with the difference between what children appear to know or are expected to know, and what they really know. *How Schools Fail* analyzes the ways in which schools foster bad strategies, raise children's fears, produce learning which is usually fragmentary, distorted, and short-lived, and generally fail to meet the real needs of children.

These four topics are clearly not exclusive. They tend to overlap and blend into each other. They are, at most, different ways of looking at and thinking about the thinking and behavior of children.

It must be made clear that the book is not about unusually bad schools or backward children. The schools in which the experiences described here took place are private schools of the highest standards and reputation. With very few exceptions, the children whose work is described are well above the average in intelligence and are, to all outward appearances, successful, and on their way to "good" secondary schools and colleges. Friends and colleagues, who understand what I am trying to say about the harmful effect of today's schooling on the character and intellect of children, and who have visited many more schools than I have, tell me that the schools I have not seen are not a bit better than those I have, and very often are worse.

Contents

STRATEGY

February 13, 1958

I can't get Nell out of my mind. When she talked
with me about fractions today, it was as if her
mind rejected understanding. Isn't this unusual?
Kids often resist understanding, make no effort to
understand; but they don't often grasp an idea
and then throw it away. Do they? But this seemed
to be what Nell was doing. Several times she
would make a real effort to follow my words, and
did follow them, through a number of steps. Then,
just as it seemed she was on the point of getting
the idea, she would shake her head and say, "I
don't get it." Can a child have a vested interest in
failure? What on earth could it be? Martha, playing the number game, often acts the same way.
She does not understand, does not want to understand, does not listen when you are explaining, and
then says, "I'm all mixed up."

There may be a connection here with *producer-
thinker* strategies. [We used the word *producer* to
describe the student who was only interested in
getting right answers, and who made more or less
uncritical use of rules and formulae to get them; we
called *thinker* the student who tried to think about

the meaning, the reality, of whatever it was he was working on.] A student who jumps at the right answer and misses often falls back into defeatism and despair because he doesn't know what else to do. The thinker is more willing to plug on.

It is surprising to hear so many of these kids say, "I'm dumb." I thought this kind of thing came later, with the bogey, adolescence. Apparently not.

My room group did fairly well today at the number game. [At certain periods, two-thirds of the class was away at art or shop classes, and the rest stayed with me for "room period," a special class, invented by Bill Hull. We met in a small room just off the classroom. There we played various kinds of intellectual games, did puzzles, and held discussions in a way as little like ordinary classroom work as possible. On this occasion we played a game like Twenty Questions, in which the teacher thinks of a number, and the students try to find it by asking questions to which the teacher may answer "Yes" or "No."] Laura was consistently the poorest asker of questions. It happened that on several occasions her turn came when the choice of numbers had been narrowed down to three or four, and she guessed the number. This made her feel that she was the official number-guesser for the day. In one game she made her first guess at an individual number where there were still twelve numbers left to choose from—obviously a poor move. Once she guessed, others started doing the same, and wasted four turns on it. Later on Mary got the idea that she was a mind reader, and started trying to guess the numbers from the beginning. The rest of her team became infected with this strategy for a while, before they went back to the plan of closing in on the number.

On the whole they were poised and collected and worked well as a team, though they didn't eliminate enough numbers at a turn. Thus, knowing that the number was between 250 and 300, they would say, "Is it between 250 and 260?" instead of taking a larger bite.

Nancy played well; but after a point the tension of the game got to be too much for her, and her mind just stopped working. She didn't get frantic, like Nell or Martha, or make fantastic guesses; she just couldn't think of anything to say, and so said nothing. A safe policy.

February 18, 1958

Intelligence is a mystery. We hear it said that most people never develop more than a very small part of their latent intellectual capacity. Probably not; but *why* not? Most of us have our engines running at about ten percent of their power. Why no more? And how do some people manage to keep revved up to twenty percent or thirty percent of their full power—or even more?

What turns the power off, or keeps it from ever being turned on?

During these past four years at the Colorado Rocky Mountain School my nose has been rubbed in the problem. When I started, I thought that some people were just born smarter than others and that not much could be done about it. This seems to be the official line of most of the psychologists. It isn't hard to believe, if all your con-

tacts with students are in the classroom or the
psychological testing room. But if you live at a
small school, seeing students in class, in the dorms,
in their private lives, at their recreations, sports,
and manual work, you can't escape the conclusion
that some people are much smarter part of the time
than they are at other times. Why? Why should
a boy or girl, who under some circumstances is
witty, observant, imaginative, analytical, in a
word, *intelligent*, come into the classroom and, as
if by magic, turn into a complete dolt?

The worst student we had, the worst I have ever
encountered, was in his life outside the classroom,
as mature, intelligent, and interesting a student
as anyone at the school. What went wrong? Experts muttered to his parents about brain damage
—a handy way to end a mystery that you can't
explain otherwise. Somewhere along the line, his
intelligence became disconnected from his schooling. Where? Why?

This past year I had some terrible students. I
failed more kids, mostly in French and Algebra,
than did all the rest of the teachers in the school
together. I did my best to get them through, good-
ness knows. Before every test we had a big cram
session of practice work, politely known as "review." When they failed the exam, we had post-
mortems, then more review, then a make-up test
(always easier than the first), which they almost
always failed again.

I thought I knew how to deal with the problem:
make the work interesting and the classroom a
lively and enthusiastic place. It was, too, some of
the time at least; many of these failing students
actually liked my classes. Overcome children's fear

of saying what they don't understand, and keep explaining until they do understand. Keep a steady and resolute pressure on them. These things I did. Result? The good students stayed good, and some may have got better; but the bad students stayed bad, and some of them seemed to get worse. If they were failing in November they were still failing in June. There must be a better answer. Maybe we can prevent kids from becoming chronic failers in the first place.

February 24, 1958

OBSERVING IN BILL HULL'S CLASS:

In today's work period three or four people came up to you for help. All were stuck on that second math problem. None of them had made any effort to listen when you were explaining it at the board. I had been watching George, who had busied himself during the explanation by trying, with a pencil, to ream and countersink a hole in the side of his desk, all the while you were talking. He indignantly denied this. I showed him the hole, which silenced him. Gerald was in dreamland; so for the most part was Nancy, though she made a good recovery when asked a question. Unusual for her. Don listened about half the time, Laura about the same. Martha amused herself by turning her hand into an animal and having it crawl around her desk.

Watching older kids study, or try to study, I saw after a while that they were not sufficiently self-aware to know when their minds had wandered off the subject. When, by speaking his name, I called a daydreamer back to earth, he was always startled, not because he had thought I wouldn't notice that he had stopped studying, but because *he* hadn't noticed.

Except by inflicting real pain on myself, I am never able to stay awake when a certain kind of sleepiness comes over me. The mind plays funny tricks at such times. I remember my own school experience of falling asleep in class while listening to the teacher's voice. I used to find that the "watchman" part of my mind that was saying, "Keep awake, you fool!" would wake me when the teacher's voice began to fade. But the part of my mind that wanted or needed sleep was not so easily beaten. It used to (and still does) counterfeit a voice, so that as I fell asleep an imaginary voice continued to sound in my head, long enough to fool me until the watchman no longer had the power to awaken me. The watchman learned, in turn, that this counterfeit voice was liable to be talking about something different, or pure nonsense, and thus learned to recognize it as counterfeit. Many times, I have dozed off with a voice sounding inside my head, only to have the watchman say, "Hey! Wake up! That voice is a phoney!"

Most of us have very imperfect control over our attention. Our minds slip away from duty before we realize that they are gone. Part of being a good student is learning to be aware of that state of one's own mind and the degree of one's own understanding. The good student may be one who often says that he does not understand, simply because he keeps a constant check on his understanding. The poor student, who does not, so to speak, watch himself trying to understand, does not know most

of the time whether he understands or not. Thus
the problem is not to get students to ask us what
they don't know; the problem is to make them
aware of the difference between what they know
and what they don't.

All this makes me think of Herb. I saw the other
day why his words so often run off the paper.
When he is copying a word, he copies about two
letters at a time. I doubt whether he looks beyond
them, or that he could tell you, in the middle of a
word, what the whole word was. He has no idea,
when he begins to copy a word, how long the
word is going to be, or how much room it may take
up.

April 21, 1958

I watched Ruth during the period of the Math
test. At least four-fifths of the time she was looking
out the window; or else she played with her pencil,
or chewed her fingernails, or looked at Nell to see
what information she might pick up. She did not
look in the least worried or confused. It looked as
if she had decided that Math tests were to be done,
not during the regular test period, when everyone
else does them, but during conference period on
Friday, with teacher close at hand, so that if she
got into a jam she could get instant help.

She seems to find the situation of not knowing
what to do so painful that she prefers to do nothing at all, waiting instead for a time when she can
call for help the moment she gets stuck. Even in
conference period today she did next to nothing.

She was trying to sneak something out of her desk. She moves rather jerkily, so every time she raised the desk lid, I saw it out of the corner of my eye and looked at her. This was rather frustrating for her; however, she kept right on trying for most of the period, not a bit abashed by being caught at it all the time.

Remember when Emily, asked to spell "microscopic," wrote MINCOPERT? That must have been several weeks ago. Today I wrote MINCOPERT on the board. To my great surprise, she recognized it. Some of the kids, watching me write it, said in amazement, "What's that for." I said, "What do you think?" Emily answered, "It's supposed to be 'microscopic.'" But she gave not the least sign of knowing that she was the person who had written MINCOPERT.

On the diagnostic spelling test, she spelled "tariff" as TEARERFIT. Today I thought I would try her again on it. This time she wrote TEARFIT. What does she do in such cases? Her reading aloud gives a clue. She closes her eyes and makes a dash for it, like someone running past a graveyard on a dark night. No looking back afterward, either.

Reminds me of a fragment of the Ancient Mariner—perhaps the world's best short ghost story:

Like one, that on a lonesome road
Doth walk in fear and dread,
And having once turned round walks on,
And turns no more his head;
Because he knows, a frightful fiend
Doth close behind him tread.

Is this the way some of these children make their way through life?

May 8, 1958

MEMO TO THE RESEARCH COMMITTEE:

I have mentioned Emily, who spelled "microscopic" MINCOPERT. She obviously made a wild grab at an answer, and having written it down, never looked at it, never checked to see if it looked right. I see a lot of this one-way, don't-look-back-it's-too-awful strategy among students. Emily in particular has shown instances of it so striking that I would like you to know about them.

Some time after the spelling test in question, I wrote MINCOPERT on the blackboard. Emily, and one other student, a good speller, interestingly enough, said that it was supposed to be "microscopic." Everyone found this very amusing, including Emily. She is a child who shows in her voice, look, coloring, and gestures much of what she is thinking, and she has not shown the least indication that she knows she is the creator of MINCOPERT. In fact, her attitude suggests that she rejects scornfully the idea that *she* would ever be so foolish as to spell the word in such a way.

Today she handed me, for display, a piece of tag board on which she had pasted some jokes that a friend had cut out of a newspaper. I found when I got to the last one that she had put the paste on the joke side, so that all there was to read was the meaningless fragment of a news

story. I was surprised that she would paste a joke
on backwards, without even looking to see whether
she had it on the right way. When it was posted,
and the other kids were looking at it, I said to
Emily, "You'll have to explain that last joke to us;
we don't get it." I thought she might look at it, for
the first time, see that it was meaningless, and
realize that she had pasted it on backside up. To
my amazement, she smiled and said with the utmost nonchalance, "As a matter of fact, I don't get
it myself." She *had* looked at it. She was perfectly
ready to accept the fact that she had posted a joke
that was meaningless. The possibility that she had
made a mistake, and that the real joke was on the
other side, did not occur to her.

I am curious about the ability of children to
turn things around in their minds. One day, in
room period, I asked the children to write on
paper certain words that I had showed them, and
then write what these would look like if seen in a
mirror. I told them to be sure to write the words
exactly as I did, with the same use of capital or
lower case letters. First I wrote CAT. Emily wrote
CAt. It didn't trouble her that two letters were
capitals, and one lower case—if she noticed it at
all. She assumed that seen in a mirror the order
of letters would be reversed, so she wroteTaC. The
lower-case *t* became capital; the *A* became lower
case. The next word was BIRD. She completely
forgot what she had just done about reversing the
order of the letters. This time she assumed that the
trick was to write each letter backwards, while
keeping them in the original order. On her paper
she had written BIrD. She reversed the *B* correctly,
wrote the *I*, then looked at the lower-case *r*, which

must have looked to her like an upside-down *L*, decided, "I must turn this right side up," and wrote *L*. Then she decided that the letters *B* and *D* should not be reversed, so her final answer was BILD. Answer to what question? She hadn't the faintest idea. Whatever task she had set out to do at the beginning had gone from her mind long before she got to the end of it; it had become changed into something else, something to do with writing letters upside down, or backwards, or something.

This child *must* be right. She cannot bear to be wrong, or even to imagine that she might be wrong. When she is wrong, as she often is, the only thing to do is to forget it as quickly as possible. Naturally she will not tell herself that she is wrong; it is bad enough when others tell her. When she is told to do something, she does it quickly and fearfully, hands it to some higher authority, and awaits the magic words, "right," or "wrong." If the word is "right," she does not have to think about that problem any more; if the word is "wrong," she does not want to, cannot bring herself to think about it.

This fear leads her to other strategies, which other children use as well. She knows that in a recitation period the teacher's attention is divided among twenty students. She also knows the teacher's strategy of asking questions of students who seem confused, or not paying attention. She therefore feels safe waving her hand in the air, as if she were bursting to tell the answer, whether she really knows it or not. This is her safe way of telling me that she, at least, knows all about whatever is going on in class. When someone else answers correctly she nods her head in emphatic agreement. Sometimes she even adds a comment, though her expression and tone of voice show that she feels this is risky. It is also interesting to note that she does not raise her hand unless there are at least half a dozen other hands up.

Sometimes she gets called on. The question arose the other day, "What is half of forty-eight?" Her hand was up; in the tiniest whisper she said, "Twenty-four." I asked her to repeat it. She said, loudly, "I said," then whispered "twenty-four." I asked her to repeat it again, because many couldn't hear her. Her face showing tension, she said, very loudly, "I said that one-half of forty-eight is . . ." and then, very softly, "twenty-four." Still, not many of the students heard. She said, indignantly, "OK, I'll shout." I said that that would be fine. She shouted, in a self-righteous tone, "The question is, what is half of forty-eight. Right?" I agreed. And once again, in a voice scarcely above a whisper, she said, "Twenty-four." I could not convince her that she had shouted the question but not the answer.

Of course, this is a strategy that often pays off. A teacher who asks a question is tuned to the right answer, ready to hear it, eager to hear it, since it will tell him that his teaching is good and that he can go on to the next topic. He will assume that anything that sounds close to the right answer is meant to be the right answer. So, for a student who is not sure of the answer, a mumble may be his best bet. If he's not sure whether something is spelled with an *a* or an *o*, he writes a letter that could be either one of them.

The mumble strategy is particularly effective in language classes. In my French classes, the stu-

dents used to work it on me, without my knowing
what was going on. It is particularly effective with
a teacher who is finicky about accents and proud
of his own. To get such a teacher to answer his
own questions is a cinch. Just make some mumbled,
garbled, hideously un-French answer, and the
teacher, with a shudder, will give the correct answer in elegant French. The student will have to
repeat it after him, but by that time he is out of
the worst danger.

Game theorists have a name for the strategy
which maximizes your chances of winning and
minimizes your losses if you should lose. They call
it "minimax." Kids are expert at finding such
strategies. They can always find ways to hedge, to
cover their bets. Not long ago, in room period, we
were working with a balance beam. A wooden arm
or beam is marked off at regular intervals and
balanced on a pivot at its midpoint. The beam can
be locked in a balanced position with a peg. We
put a weight at a chosen point on one side of the
beam, then give the student another weight,
perhaps the same, perhaps heavier, perhaps lighter,
which he is to place on the other side of the beam
so that, when the beam is unlocked, it will stay in
the balanced position. When a student has placed
the weight, the other members of his group say, in
turn, whether they think the beam will balance or
not.

One day it was Emily's turn to place the weight.
After much thought, she placed it wrongly. One
by one, the members of the group said that they
thought it would not balance. As each one spoke,
she had less and less confidence in her choice.
Finally, when they had all spoken and she had to

unlock the beam, she looked around and said brightly, "I don't think it's going to balance either, personally." Written words can not convey the tone of her voice: she had completely dissociated herself from that foolish person (whoever it was) who had placed the weight on such a ridiculous spot. When she pulled the peg and the beam swung wildly, she almost seemed to feel vindicated. Most of the children hedge their bets, but few do it so unashamedly, and some even seem to feel that there is something dishonorable in having so little courage of your own convictions.

May 10, 1958

Children are often quite frank about the strategies they use to get answers out of a teacher. I once observed a class in which the teacher was testing her students on parts of speech. On the blackboard she had three columns, headed Noun, Adjective, and Verb. As she gave each word, she called on a child and asked in which column the word belonged.

Like most teachers, she hadn't thought enough about what she was doing to realize, first, that many of the words given could fit into more than one column; and secondly, that it is often the way a word is used that determines what part of speech it is.

There was a good deal of the tried-and-true strategy of *guess-and-look*, in which you start to say a word, all the while scrutinizing the teacher's face to see whether you are on the right track or not. With most teachers, no further strategies are needed. This one was more poker-faced than most, so *guess-and-look* wasn't working very well. Still, the percentage of hits was remarkably high, especially since it was clear to me from the way the children were talking and acting that they hadn't a notion of what Nouns, Adjectives, and Verbs were. Finally one child said, "Miss—, you shouldn't point to the answer each time." The teacher was surprised, and asked what she meant. The child said, "Well, you don't exactly *point*, but you kind of stand next to the answer." This was no clearer, since the teacher had been standing still. But after a while, as the class went on, I thought I saw what the girl meant. Since the teacher wrote each word down in its proper column, she was, in a way, getting herself ready to write, pointing herself at the place where she would soon be writing. From the angle of her body to the blackboard the children picked up a subtle clue to the correct answer.

This was not all. At the end of every third word, her three columns came out even, that is, there were an equal number of nouns, adjectives, and verbs. This meant that when she started off a new row, you had one chance in three of getting the right answer by a blind guess; but for the next word, you had one chance in two, and the last word was a dead giveaway to the lucky student who was asked it. Hardly any missed this opportunity; in fact, they answered so quickly that the teacher (brighter than most) caught on to their system and began keeping her columns uneven, making the strategist's job a bit harder.

In the midst of all this, there came a vivid example of the kind of thing we say in school that makes no sense, that only bewilders and confuses the thoughtful child who tries to make sense out of it. The teacher, whose specialty, by the way, was English, had told these children that a verb is a word of action—which is not always true. One of the words she asked was "dream." She was thinking of the noun, and apparently did not remember that "dream" can as easily be a verb. One little boy, making a pure guess, said it was a verb. Here the teacher, to be helpful, contributed one of those "explanations" that are so much more hindrance than help. She said, "But a verb has to have action; can you give me a sentence, using 'dream', that has action?" The child thought a bit, and said, "I had a dream about the Trojan War." Now it's pretty hard to get much more action than that. But the teacher told him he was wrong, and he sat silent, with an utterly baffled and frightened expression on his face. She was so busy thinking about what she wanted him to say, she was so obsessed with that *right answer* hidden in her mind, that she could not think about what he was really saying and thinking, could not see that his reasoning was logical and correct, and that the mistake was not his, but hers.

At one of our leading prep schools I saw, the other day, an example of the way in which a teacher may not know what is going on in his own class.

This was a math class. The teacher, an experienced man, was doing the day's assignment on the blackboard. His way of keeping attention was to ask various members of the class, as he did each step, "Is that right?" It was a dull class, and I found it hard to keep my mind on it. It seemed to me that most students in the class had their minds elsewhere, with a mental sentry posted to alert them when their names were called. As each name was called, the boy who was asked if something or other was right answered "Yes." The class droned on. In time my mind slipped away altogether, I don't know for how long. Suddenly something snapped me to attention. I looked at the teacher. Every boy in the class was looking at him, too. The boy who had been asked if what had just been written was right, was carefully looking at the blackboard. After a moment he said, "No, sir, that isn't right, it ought to be so-and-so." The teacher chuckled appreciatively and said, "You're right, it should be." He made the change, and the class and I settled back into our private thoughts for the rest of the period.

After the boys had left, I thanked the teacher for letting me visit. He said, "You notice I threw them a little curve ball there. I do that every now and then. Keeps them on their toes." I said something in agreement. It didn't seem the time or place to tell him that when he threw his little curve ball the expression in his voice changed enough so that it warned, not only the boys, but also a complete stranger, that something was coming up and that attention had better be paid.

July 7, 1958

I've been reading over all the memos from last winter and spring. It is a curious and unsettling process, the business of changing your mind on a subject about which you had very positive convictions. After all I have said and written about the need for keeping children under pressure, I find myself coming to realize that what hampers their thinking, what drives them into these narrow and defensive strategies, is a feeling that they must please the grownups at all costs. The really able thinkers in our class turn out to be, without exception, children who don't feel so strongly the need to please grownups. Some of them are good students, some not so good; but good or not, they don't work to please us, but to please themselves.

Here is Walter, just the opposite, very eager to do whatever people want him to do, and very good at doing it. (By conventional standards he was a very able pupil, so much so that people called him brilliant, which he most assuredly was not.)

We had the problem, "If you are travelling at 40 miles per hour, how long will it take you to go 10 miles?"

Walter: 4 minutes.

JH (me): How did you get it?

W: Divided the 40 by the 10.

A quick look at my face told him that this would not do. After a while he wrote, "15 minutes." I wanted to check his understanding.

JH: If you were going 50 miles per hour, how far would you go in 24 minutes?

W (quickly): 36 miles.

JH: How did you get that?

W: Subtracted 24 from 60.

He still hadn't gotten it. I tried again.

JH: If you were going 50 miles per hour, how far would you go in 30 minutes?

W: 25 miles. 30 minutes is half an hour, and half of 50 is 25.

It sounded as if he knew what he was doing at last. I thought he would have no trouble with the 24 minutes problem. But it took a long time, with some hinting from me, before he saw that 24 minutes was 2/5 of an hour, and therefore, that he would go 2/5 of 50 miles, or 20 miles, in 24 minutes. Would he have discovered it if I had not paved the way with leading questions? Hard to tell.

Most teachers would have assumed, as I would have once, that when he got the 15-minutes problem, he knew what he was doing. Even the skeptical would have been convinced when he gave his explanation about the 30-minutes problem. Yet in each case he showed that he had not really understood what he was doing, and it is not at all certain that he understands yet.

What was his strategy here? Certainly he was numeral shoving. More than that, he was making up a fairly sensible sounding explanation of how he was doing the problem. And yet, is it not possible, even probable, that in saying that in half an hour you go half of 50 miles, he was merely doing some word shoving to go along with his numeral shoving? The explanation sounded reasonable to me, because, in this case, his way of shoving the numerals happened to be the right way; but he was just as happy with his explanations when he was shoving the numerals the wrong way.

This is a disquieting thought. We say and believe that at this school we teach children to understand the meaning of what they do in math. How? By giving them (and requiring them to give back to us) "explanations" of what they do. But let's take a child's-eye view. Might not a child feel, as Walter obviously did, that in this school you not only have to get the right answer, but you also have to have the right explanation to go with it; the right answer, and the right chatter. Yet we see here that a "successful" student can give the answer and the chatter without understanding at all what he was doing or saying.

July 25, 1958

OBSERVING IN BILL HULL'S CLASS:

Of all I saw and learned this past half-year, one thing stands out. What goes on in class is not what teachers think—certainly not what I had always thought. For years now I have worked with a picture in mind of what my class was like. This reality, which I felt I knew, was partly physical, partly mental or spiritual. In other words, I thought I knew, in general, what the students were doing, and also what they were thinking and feeling. I see now that my picture of reality was almost wholly false. Why didn't I see this before?

Sitting at the side of the room, watching these kids, not so much to check up on them as to find out what they were like and how they differed from the teen-agers I have worked with and know, I slowly became aware of something. You can't find out what a child does in class by looking at him only when he is called on. You have to watch him for long stretches of time without his knowing it.

During many of the recitation classes, when the class supposedly is working as a unit, most of the children paid very little attention to what was going on. Those who most needed to pay attention, usually paid the least. The kids who knew the answer to whatever question you were asking wanted to make sure that you knew they knew, so their hands were always waving. Also, knowing the right answer, they were in a position to enjoy to the full the ridiculous answers that might be given by their less fortunate colleagues. But, as in all classes, these able students are a minority. What of the unsuccessful majority? Their attention depended on what was going on in class. Any raising of the emotional temperature made them prick up their ears. If an argument was going on, or someone was in trouble, or someone was being laughed at for a foolish answer, they took notice. Or, if you were explaining to a slow student something so simple that all the rest knew it, they would wave their arms and give agonized, half-suppressed cries of "O-o-o-o-oh ! O-o-o-o-oh !" But most of the time, when explaining, questioning, or discussing was going on, the majority of children paid little attention or none at all. Some day-dreamed, and no amount of calling them back to earth with a crash, much as it amused everyone else, could break them of the habit. Others wrote and passed notes, or whispered, or held conversations in sign language, or made doodles or pictures on their papers or desks, or fiddled with objects.

There doesn't seem to be much a teacher can do about this, if he is really teaching and not just keeping everyone quiet and busy. A teacher in class is like a man in the woods at night with a powerful flashlight in his hand. Wherever he turns his light, the creatures on whom it shines are aware of it, and do not behave as they do in the dark. Thus the mere fact of his watching their behavior changes it into something very different. Shine where he will, he can never know very much of the night life of the woods.

So, in class, the teacher can turn the spotlight of his attention, now on this child, now on that, now on them all; but the children know when his attention is on them, and do not act at all as they do when it is elsewhere. A teacher who is really thinking about what a particular child is doing or asking, or about what he, himself, is trying to explain, will not be able to know what all the rest of the class is doing. And if he does notice that other children are doing what they should not, and tells them to stop, they know they have only to wait until he gets back, as he must, to his real job. Classroom observers don't seem to see much of this. Why not? Some of them do not stay with a class long enough for the children to begin to act naturally in their presence. But even those who are with a class for a long time make the mistake of watching the teacher too much and the children too little. Student teachers in training spend long periods of time in one classroom, but they think they are in there to learn *How To Teach*, to pick up the tricks of child management from watching a *Master At Work*. Their concern is with manipulating and controlling children rather than understanding them. So they watch the teacher, see only what the teacher sees, and thus lose most of what could be a valuable experience.

There should be more situations in which two experienced teachers share the same class, teaching and observing the same group of kids, thinking, and talking to each other, about what they see and hear. Schools can't afford to support this; they can barely pay the one teacher in each class. I should think foundations might be willing to support this kind of work. They seem ready at the drop of a hat to spend millions of dollars on grandiose projects which produce, in the main, only publicity and doctoral dissertations. Perhaps they feel that to have two teachers learn a great deal more about children than they knew before is not worth spending money on. If so, I think they're wrong. When I think what this year's experience has revealed about children's work, behavior, and thought, what avenues of exploration and speculation it has opened up, I can only wonder what extraordinary discoveries about learning might be made if other teachers in other places could work in this way.

July 27, 1958

It has become clear over the year that these children see school almost entirely in terms of the day-to-day and hour-to-hour tasks that we impose on them. This is not at all the way the teacher thinks of it. The conscientious teacher thinks of himself as taking his students (at least part way) on a journey to some glorious destination, well worth the pains of the trip. If he teaches history, he thinks how interesting, how exciting, how useful it is to know history, and how fortunate his students will be when they begin to share his knowledge. If he teaches French, he thinks of the glories of French literature, or the beauty of spoken French, or the delights of French cooking, and how he is helping to make these joys available to his students. And so for all subjects.

Thus teachers feel, as I once did, that their interests and their students' are fundamentally the same. I used to feel that I was guiding and helping my students on a journey that they wanted to take but could not take without my help. I knew the way looked hard, but I assumed they could see the goal almost as clearly as I and that they were almost as eager to reach it. It seemed very important to give students this feeling of being on a journey to a worthwhile destination. I see now that most of my talk to this end was wasted breath. Maybe *I* thought the students were in my class because they were eager to learn what I was trying to teach, but they knew better. They were in school because they had to be, and in my class either because they had to be, or because otherwise they would have had to be in another class, which might be even worse.

Children in school are like children at the doctor's. He can talk himself blue in the face about how much good his medicine is going to do them; all they think of is how much it will hurt or how bad it will taste. Given their own way, they would have none of it.

So the valiant and resolute band of travelers I thought I was leading toward a much-hoped-for destination turned out instead to be more like convicts in a chain gang, forced under threat of punishment to move along a rough path leading nobody knew where and down which they could see hardly more than a few steps ahead. School feels like this to children: it is a place where *they* make you go and where *they* tell you to do things and where *they* try to make your life unpleasant if you don't do them or don't do them right.

For children, the central business of school is not learning, whatever this vague word means; it is getting these daily tasks done, or at least out of the way, with a minimum of effort and unpleasantness. Each task is an end in itself. The children don't care how they dispose of it. If they can get it out of the way by doing it, they will do it; if experience has taught them that this does not work very well, they will turn to other means, illegitimate means, that wholly defeat whatever purpose the task-giver may have had in mind.

They are very good at this, at getting other people to do their tasks for them. I remember the day not long ago when Ruth opened my eyes. We had been doing math, and I was pleased with myself because, instead of telling her answers and showing her how to do problems, I was "making her think" by asking her questions. It was slow work. Question after question met only silence. She said nothing, did nothing, just sat and looked at me through those glasses, and waited. Each time, I had to think of a question easier and more pointed than the last, until I finally found one so easy that she would feel safe in answering it. So we inched our way along until suddenly, looking at her as I waited for an answer to a question, I saw with a start that she was not at all puzzled by what I had asked her. In fact, she was not even thinking about it. She was coolly appraising me, weighing my patience, waiting for that next, sure-to-be-easier question. I thought, "I've been had!" The girl had learned how to make me do her work for her, just as she had learned to make all her previous teachers do the same thing. If I wouldn't tell her the answers, very well, she would just let me question her right up to them.

Schools and teachers seem generally to be as blind to children's strategies as I was. Otherwise, they would teach their courses and assign their tasks so that students who really thought about the meaning of the subject would have the best chance of succeeding, while those who tried to do the tasks by illegitimate means, without thinking or understanding, would be foiled. But the reverse seems to be the case. Schools give every encouragement to *producers*, the kids whose idea is to get "right answers" by any and all means. In a system that runs on "right answers," they can hardly help it. And these schools are often very discouraging places for *thinkers*.

Until recently it had not occurred to me that poor students thought differently about their work than good students; I assumed they thought the same way, only less skillfully. Now it begins to look as if the expectation and fear of failure, if strong enough, may lead children to act and think in a special way, to adopt strategies different from those of more confident children. Emily is a good example. She is emotionally as well as intellectually incapable of checking her work, of comparing her ideas against reality, of making any kind of judgment about the value of her thoughts. She makes me think of an animal fleeing danger—go like the wind, don't look back, remember where that danger was, and stay away from it as far as you can. Are there many other children who react to their fears in this way?

September 22, 1958

It doesn't take children long to figure out their teachers. Some of these kids already know that what pays off with us is plenty of talk, lots of ideas, even if they are wild. What can we do for the kids who may like to think but don't like to talk?

In my math classes I am on the horns of another dilemma. I want the kids to think about what they are doing. If I make the questions too hard, they begin trying to read my mind, or, as they did this morning, they throw out wild ideas, taking all too literally my statement that a wrong idea is better than none. If, on the other hand, I break the subject down into little lumps, so that when I ask a question most of the class will be able to answer with confidence, am I not doing what I found I was doing for Ruth last year, doing most of their thinking for them?

Perhaps there is no middle position, and what I must do is ask hard questions some of the time, easy questions other times.

October 13, 1958

What the sixth-grade teachers said the other day suggests that some of our last year's strategists have not reformed. Let's not be too discouraged about this. Given these children whose strategies are short-sighted and self-defeating, these answer-grabbers and teacher-pleasers, we can to some extent, and over a long period of time, create situations in which some of them may be willing to use their minds in better ways. Some of these, in turn, may even carry these new ways of thinking into a new situation; but we can't expect that they all will. Most of them will probably drop back into the strategies with which they are most familiar and comfortable.

Not many children, in one school year, are going to remake their whole way of dealing with life. With luck, we can give some of them a feeling of what it is like to turn one's full intelligence on a problem, to think creatively, originally, and constructively instead of defensively and evasively. We can hope that they will enjoy the experience enough to want to try it again; but it is only a hope. To put it another way, we can try to give them a glimpse of an intellectual foreign country, and even persuade them to visit it for a while; but it would take more time than we have to make them citizens of that country.

There's no telling what might be done with children if, from their very first days in school, we concentrated on creating the conditions in which intelligence was most likely to grow. Of course, setting up the conditions under which good thinking can be done does not always mean that it will be done.

Take Sam. He seems temperamentally ready to think well, but he rarely does. The other day I had some number series on the board, and asked the class to tell me any relationships they could see in them. Sam's first two or three observations were of this order: "There's a one in the top line and a one in the middle line, and there's a two in the third number and a two in the fifth number. . . ." Very trivial, very local, no generality among them at all. Then, in the middle of all this, he came up with a very powerful generalization that I had not even seen myself.

The funny thing is that I don't think he felt that one of these ideas was any better than another. He might one day say that horses and cows were similar in that they were domestic farm animals that ate grass; and the next day that they were alike because he had never ridden on either, or something like that. How can we help him to see that some ways of looking at things, ordering things, are more useful than others?

We have to convince the children that they must not be afraid to ask questions; but further than that, we must get across the idea that some questions are more useful than others, and that to the right kind of question the answer "No" can be as revealing as "Yes." Here is where Twenty Questions, the card game, the balance beam, all come in handy. The scientist who asks a question of nature—*i.e.* performs an experiment—tries to ask one such that he will gain information whichever way his experiment comes out, and will have an idea of what to do next. He asks his questions with a purpose. This is a subtle art. Can fifth graders learn some of it?

When Nancy and Sheila worked the balance beam last year, they were often close to the truth, but they could never hang onto it because they could never express their ideas in a form they could test with an experiment. Once one of them said, "Things weigh more further out." This was a big step; but they couldn't think of a way to check or refine this insight, they couldn't ask themselves (to use their terms) how much more things weigh when they get further out.

December 7, 1958

Some of our strategists at work:

Atlas Paper #2 asks the students, "What two key words on each index page of the Atlas tell at a glance which names can be found on that page?" The students are supposed to notice that the first and the last place names on any page are printed in larger type at the top of the page—as in a dictionary. The other day, Abby and Jane could not understand what the instructions were asking them to do, largely because they were too busy thinking about the answer to be able to think about the instructions. We studied the examples given in the paper, but to no avail. Finally I told them to sit at their desks and think about it some more. A minute or two later Jane appeared at the door and said indignantly, "Are you *sure* that it isn't those two words at the top of the page?" Having said no such thing, I was taken aback, and said with some surprise, "When did I say that?" She immediately turned to Abby, who was waiting outside the door, and said, "Write it down!" She had all the clues she needed.

March 21, 1959

Here are some of the children working on the balance beam experiment (described in the memo of May 8, 1958). One child has placed the weight where he thinks it will balance the beam; the others are being asked to predict whether it will balance.

Abby: It might move a little to one side—not much.

Elaine: It might teeter a little, then balance, but not really. (She really is covering all the possibilities.)

Rachel: It might balance.

Pat: It will balance pretty much.

Elaine: Teeter totter a teeny bit, then balance.

In this next example, 4 x 5″ means that we put four weights five inches out on the beam. 2 x ? means that we gave the child 2 weights to place. In this case, 2 x 10″ would have made the beam balance.

4 x 5″; 2 x ? Elaine put them at 2″, then at 1″, then at 9″. I asked, "Is that your choice?" She said, "Yes, but I don't think it will balance." The object of the experiment was to make it balance! She decided to leave the weights at 9″.

Asked if it would balance, Hester said, "Somehow I think it might."

8 x 2″; 4 x ?

Rachel (moving the weights back and forth without conviction): Probably won't balance.

Barbara: Put them where you think it *will*. (Barbara is one of our few positive strategists, and so in everything she does.)

Rachel put the weights at 1″. Needless to say, the beam did not balance.

3 x 2″ ; 6 x ? Hester scattered the six blocks all over the beam, as if in the hope that one of them might hit the magic spot.

Barbara's turn. Everyone will predict that the beam will balance.

2 x 3″ ; 1 x ? First she put them at 5″. She is counting out lines instead of spaces. Then she saw her mistake, and put them at 6″. Everyone except Hester said Yes, the beam would balance.

1 x 10″ ; 2 x ?

Barbara: 2 x 5″. Then she said confidently but with some excitement in her voice, "It's going to do it!"

Elaine: You put a block here (1″), it makes it lighter; here (5″) makes it heavier.

When his turn came, Garry said, "I think it's just going to go down—that's safer."

1 x 10″ ; 1 x ? Betty put the weight at 10″.

Gil: May go down a little and then come back up.

Garry: It will be about even.

Betty: I sort of think it's going to balance.

4 x 6″; 4 x ? Ralph put them at 6″. But two members of the group predicted that it would not balance; then Betty spoke up: "I'll say it will, just in case it does, so we won't get too low a score.' Talk about Minimax!

Our way of scoring was to give the groups a point for each correct prediction. Before long they were thinking more of ways to get a good score than of making the beam balance. We wanted them to figure out how to balance the beam, and introduced the scoring as a matter of motivation. But they outsmarted us, and figured out ways to get a good score that had nothing to do with whether the beam balanced or not.

4 x 9″, 4 x ? Sam put them at 9″. Ralph said, "He

didn't trust me, but I'm going to trust him, because that's where I would have put it."

Later, Sam said to another player, "Do what you think is right." To which Betty, usually a positive character, said, "Play safe."

At about this point Betty figured out that the way to get a good score was to put the weights in what you know is a wrong place, and then have everyone on your team say that it is wrong. Thus they will each get a point for predicting correctly. Later, Nat said, "Are *no* votes just as good as *yes* votes?" It was a good question; we should have made *yes* votes count much more.

Another group working.

$4 \times 8''$; $4 \times$? Tony put them at $7''$, then said, "Get ready to disagree." Then he changed them to $8''$. All predicted *yes*, but Nat hedged.

Later, when it was his turn to predict, Nat said, "Too bad you have to be so specific."

April 28, 1959

Here are some notes from the other day, when the fourth graders were playing Twenty Questions.

Many of them are very anxious when their turn comes to ask a question. We ask them to play Twenty Questions in the hope that, wanting to find the hidden thought, they will learn to ask more informative and useful questions.

They see the game quite differently: "When my turn comes, I have to ask a question." They are not the least interested in the object of the game, or whether their question gains useful information.

The problem is simply to think of a question, any old question. The first danger is that you will just be sitting there, unable to think of a question. The next danger is that when you ask a question, other kids will think it is silly, laugh at it, say, "That's no good."

So the problem becomes not just thinking up a question, but thinking up a question that will sound good. The best way to do this is to listen to kids that you know are pretty sharp, and ask questions that sound like theirs. Thus, a child who found in one game that "Is it water?" was a useful question, went on asking it in game after game, even when other questions had established that the information sought for had nothing to do with water.

Many of our kids play the same way. Pat, Rachel, and some others never have any idea what the object of the game is, or what information has been gained by questions already asked. All they want, when their turn comes, is to have a question that won't be laughed at. Jessie plays it even safer than that. She just refuses to ask a question, says, "I pass," and looks very pleased with herself after she says it, too.

Another popular strategy is the disguised blind guess. When kids first play this game, every question is a guess. Then some of them see that it is silly to guess right at the beginning, and that the sensible thing to do is narrow down the possibilities. They criticize very severely teammates who start guessing too soon. So the trick becomes to ask a guessing question that doesn't sound like a guess, like Nat's classic, "Was he killed by Brutus?" This has become something of a joke in his group. Still, every question he asks conceals a guess.

One day we were using the atlas, and the field of the game was geographical locations. Sam wanted to ask if it was Italy, but that was a guess, so he said, "Does it look like a boot?" Every time it is his turn, he says, "Can I make a guess?" The strategy of narrowing down possibilities has not occurred to him, or if it has, he does not know how to make use of it.

Betty makes multiple guesses. Thinking of either Corsica or Sardinia, she asked, "Does it begin with C or S?" Another time she said, "Does it begin with B, D, C, P, or T?" This is not bad strategy. On another occasion she said to a cautious teammate, "Don't say 'Could it be?'; say 'Is it?' " She's a positive little critter.

Sometimes we try to track down a number with Twenty Questions. One day I said I was thinking of a number between 1 and 10,000. Children who use a good narrowing-down strategy to find a number between 1 and 100, or 1 and 500, go all to pieces when the number is between 1 and 10,000. Many start guessing from the very beginning. Even when I say that the number is very large, they will try things like 65, 113, 92. Other kids will narrow down until they find that the number is in the 8,000's; then they start guessing, as if there were now so few numbers to choose from that guessing became worthwhile. Their confidence in these shots in the dark is astonishing. They say, "We've got it this time!" They are always incredulous when they find they have not got it.

They still cling stubbornly to the idea that the only good answer is a *yes* answer. This, of course, is the result of their miseducation, in which "right answers" are the only ones that pay off. They have not learned how to learn from a mistake, or even that learning from mistakes is possible. If they say, "Is the number between 5,000 and 10,000?" and I say *yes*, they cheer; if I say *no*, they groan, even though they get exactly the same amount of information in either case. The more anxious ones will, over and over again, ask questions that have already been answered, just for the satisfaction of hearing a *yes*. Their more sophisticated teammates point out in vain that it is silly to ask a question when you already know the answer.

FEAR AND FAILURE

March 27, 1958

We agree that all children need to succeed; but do we mean the same thing? My own feeling is that success should not be quick or easy, and should not come all the time. Success implies overcoming an obstacle, including, perhaps, the thought in our minds that we might not succeed. It is turning, "I can't" into "I can, and I did."

We ought also to learn, beginning early, that we don't always succeed. A good batting average in baseball is .300; a good batting average in life is a great deal lower than that. Life holds many more defeats than victories for all of us. Shouldn't we get used to this early? We should learn, too, to aim higher than we think we can hit. "A man's reach should exceed his grasp, or what's a Heaven for?" What we fail to do today, we, or someone, may do tomorrow. Our failure may pave the way for someone else's success.

Of course we should protect a child, if we can, from a diet of unbroken failure. More to the point, perhaps, we should see that failure is honorable and constructive, rather than humiliating. Perhaps we need a semantic distinction here, between non-success and failure.

It is tempting to think that we can arrange the work of unsuccessful students so that they think they are succeeding most of the time. But how can we keep secret from a child what other children of his own age, in his own or other schools, are doing? What some of these kids need is the experience of doing something really well—so well that they know themselves, without having to be told, that they have done it well. Maybe this means that someone must supply them, from outside, with the concentration and resolution they lack.

December 3, 1958

The other day I decided to talk to the other section about what happens when you don't understand what is going on. We had been chatting about something or other, and everyone seemed in a relaxed frame of mind, so I said, "You know, there's something I'm curious about, and I wonder if you'd tell me." They said, "What?" I said, "What do you think, what goes through your mind, when the teacher asks you a question and you don't know the answer?"

It was a bombshell. Instantly a paralyzed silence fell on the room. Everyone stared at me with what I have learned to recognize as a tense expression. For a long time there wasn't a sound. Finally Ben, who is bolder than most, broke the tension, and also answered my question, by saying in a loud voice, "Gulp!"

He spoke for everyone. They all began to

clamor, and all said the same thing, that when
the teacher asked them a question and they didn't
know the answer they were scared half to death. I
was flabbergasted—to find this in a school which
people think of as progressive; which does its best *fear*
not to put pressure on little children; which does *fear*
not give marks in the lower grades; which tries to *fear*
keep children from feeling that they're in some
kind of race. *fear*

I asked them why they felt gulpish. They said
they were afraid of failing, afraid of being kept
back, afraid of being called stupid, afraid of feel- *stupid*
ing themselves stupid. Stupid. Why is it such a *stupid*
deadly insult to these children, almost the worst
thing they can think of to call each other? Where
do they learn this?

Even in the kindest and gentlest of schools,
children are afraid, many of them a great deal of
the time, some of them almost all the time. This is
a hard fact of life to deal with. What can we do
about it?

December 30, 1958

All fall long, I wondered why Jack fell down so
much playing soccer. He is an agile, well-coor-
dinated boy. His balance is good. People don't
knock him over. Why was he on the ground so
often? Suddenly, the other day, I had the answer.

I discovered it while trying to learn to control
the tension that builds up in me when I practice
the flute. Music is a good thing for teachers to
study, because it creates in us the kind of tension
that children live under all the time in the class-

room, and that most adults have long forgotten.
Incidentally, it is most interesting, when Gattegno
explains the Cuisenaire rods[1] to teachers, to see
them under this very tension. They react to it very
much like children, by getting sore at Gattegno, or
fighting his ideas, by saying in elaborate language
what fifth graders say when they are startled by a
new idea—"This is crazy, nutty, cuckoo."

I have observed many times that children who
can do one or two problems of a certain kind,
with no trouble, collapse when given a big sheet
of them. Something like this is true of exercises in
music. When I am trying to play an exercise at
(for me) high speed, I am under tension. If the
exercise is short, I feel that I can get through it
before tension gets the better of me. But if it is
long, I am less confident from the start that I can
get through without a mistake, and as I play, the
inner voice that comments on what I am doing
says: "All right so far; watch that G sharp; oops!
narrow escape, you almost played F sharp instead
of F natural, etc., etc." The voice gets louder and
louder, until finally the communication channels
are clogged up, coordination breaks down, and I
make the mistake I have been fearing to make.

I haven't forgotten Jack and his falling down.
One thing I have discovered is that there is a
peculiar kind of relief, a lessening of tension, when
you make a mistake. For when you make one, you
no longer have to worry about whether you are
going to make one. Walking a tightrope, you worry
about falling off; once fallen off, you don't have to
worry. Children, to whom making mistakes is

[1] See footnote, pp. 106-107.

acutely painful, are therefore under great tension
when doing something correctly. Worrying about
the mistakes they might make is as bad—no, worse
—than worrying about the mistakes they have
made. Thus, when you tell a child that he has
done a problem wrong, you often hear a sigh of
relief. He says, "I *knew* it would be wrong." He
would rather *be* wrong, and know it, than not know
whether he was wrong or not.

Well, the reason Jack falls down is that this
relieves him, for a few seconds, of the great tension he is under when he plays soccer. Being
small, he is afraid of crashing into bigger boys, but
he is also afraid of showing his fear, and resolutely
tries to play the game as he feels he should. This
puts his nervous system under a strain that is too
much for it. Being a boy, he can't pull out of the
game, as a girl might do, or just get out of the way
of bigger boys when they come at him. So, every
now and then, he falls down, and thus gets an
honorable rest period for a second or two.

This makes me think about written work. Some
say that children get security from large amounts
of written work. Maybe. But suppose every teacher
in the school were told that he had to do ten pages
of addition problems, within a given time limit and
with no mistakes, or lose his job. Even if the time
given were ample enough to do all problems carefully with time over for checking, the chances are
that no teacher would get a perfect paper. Their
anxiety would build up, as it does in me when I
play the flute, until it impaired or wholly broke
down their coordination and confidence. Have you
ever found yourself, while doing a simple arithmetic problem, checking the answer over and over, as

if you could not believe that you had done it right? I have. If we were under the gun as much as the kids in our classes are, we would do this more often.

Perhaps children need a lot of written work, particularly in math; but they should not get much of it at one time. Ask children to spend a whole period on one paper, and anxiety or boredom is sure to drive them into foolish errors. It used to puzzle me that the students who made the most mistakes and got the worst marks were so often the first ones to hand in their papers. I used to say, "If you finish early, take time to check your work, do some problems again." Typical teacher's advice; I might as well have told them to flap their arms and fly. When the paper was in, the tension was ended. Their fate was in the lap of the gods. They might still worry about flunking the paper, but it was a fatalistic kind of worry, it didn't contain the agonizing element of choice, there was nothing more they could do about it. Worrying about whether you did the right thing, while painful enough, is less painful than worrying about the right thing to do.

One way to keep down tension is to be aware of it. I told the math class that to let something go by in class without knowing what it means, and without saying anything, is like leaving something in Howard Johnson's on a long car trip. You are going to have to go back for it eventually, so the sooner the better. This foolish metaphor has helped the kids, or so they say. They have learned to recognize, if only a little, the feeling of panicky confusion that slowly gets hold of them. To be able to say, "I'm getting left at Howard Johnson's" helps them to control this feeling, and if it gets too much for them they can always tell me that they have been left behind; then I can do something about picking them up.

We must set a limit to the tension that we put children under. If we don't, they will set their own limits by not paying attention, by fooling around, by saying unnecessarily, "I don't get it." We should let them know in advance that they will not have to be under tension for an entire period, and that, if need be, they have the means to bring it to a stop.

Perhaps this is a reason why people like Gattegno, who go around teaching demonstration math classes, get such spectacular results. The kids know that this is not real school, that this strange man is not their teacher, that if they make mistakes nothing serious will happen, and that, in any case, it will be over soon. Thus freed from worrying, they are ready to use their brains. But how can we run a class from day to day and keep that spirit? Can it be done at all?

February 5, 1959

How is it possible for children of only ten to have such strongly developed concepts of themselves, and these unfavorable almost to the point of self-contempt and self-hatred? We expect this of older children; but that it should have gone so far, so soon . . .

Are there any of them who are so busy with the world and with living that they just don't bother to think much about themselves? Perhaps Betty.

Perhaps Hal. Not many others.

Perhaps they are thrown too early, and too much, into a crowded society of other children, where they have to think, not about the world, but about their position in it.

Is it possible that our modern way of teaching, all gentleness, persuasiveness, and human contact, tends to make children get themselves and their work all mixed up? The first school I went to was very different from this. Even when I was five, the teachers there never called me anything but Holt. Of me, as a person, they seemed to take little notice. I didn't know whether they liked me or not; it never occurred to me to wonder. My work was what concerned them. If it was good, it was commended; if bad, it was criticized. There may be more than we think in this old-fashioned way of dealing with children. Maybe it was easier for children to grow up in a world in which, when they impinged on the world of adults, they were treated firmly, impersonally, and ceremoniously, but were otherwise left alone.

There was a word on Sam's report card that he could not understand; he was almost in tears over it. Why should he have *assumed* that it was bad? Of course, we adults tend to see all small, specific failures, of our own or of children, as proof of general failure, incompetence, worthlessness. Is it a cultural matter? Are there no people in the world for whom it is *not* a disgrace to do something badly?

Note the danger of using a child's concept of himself to get him to do good work. We say "You are the kind of sensible, smart, good, etc., etc. boy or girl who can easily do this problem, if you try."

But if the work fails, so does the concept. If he can't do the problem, no matter how hard he tries, then, clearly, he is not sensible, smart, or good.

If children worry so much about failure, might it not be because they rate success too highly and depend on it too much? May there not be altogether too much praise for good work in the lower grades? If, when Johnny does good work, we make him feel "good," may we not, without intending it, be making him feel "bad" when he does bad work?

Do children really need so much praise? When a child, after a long struggle, finally does the cube puzzle, does he need to be told that he has done well? Doesn't he know, without being told, that he has accomplished something? In fact, when we praise him, are we not perhaps horning in on his accomplishment, stealing a little of his glory, edging our way into the limelight, praising ourselves for having helped to turn out such a smart child? Is not *most* adult praise of children a kind of self-praise? I think of that marvelous composition that Nat wrote about the dining room in his house. I find now, to my horror, that in thinking with satisfaction about that comp, I am really congratulating myself for my part in it. What a clever boy this is! and what a clever man am I for helping to make him so!

February 11, 1959

Someone asked the other day, "Why do we go to school?" Pat, with a vigor unusual in her, said "So when we grow up we won't be stupid." These children equate stupidity with ignorance. Is this what they mean when they call themselves stupid? Is this one of the reasons why they are so ashamed of not knowing something? If so, have we, perhaps unknowingly, taught them to feel this way? We should clear up this distinction, show them that it is possible to know very few facts, but make very good use of them. Conversely, one can know many facts and still act stupidly. The learned fool is by no means rare in this country.

April 24, 1959

Strategy is an outgrowth of character. Children use the strategies they do because of the way they feel, the expectations they have of the universe, the way they evaluate themselves, the classroom, and the demands made on them. Rachel sees the class as a place where she is told to do certain things, praised if she does them right, disapproved of if she does not. She is not likely to use good strategy no matter how much we press it on her. Even if I give her problems which she must think about to solve, and even if she thinks about them and solves them, which hardly ever happens, she will make of this a kind of production strategy. She will say, as I think she does say, that this is a crazy class and that this screwball is always giving her funny kinds of problems to puzzle over; but she will not carry this way of working on problems over into other work, or into the main part of her life. Her first concern will still be self-defense.

One thing we see in our intelligent children is that they are intensely involved with life. Rachel,

Pat, Elaine, Garry, all are daydreamers. But Barbara, Betty, Maria, Ralph, and Hal don't withdraw from life; they embrace it. We spoke once of a love affair with learning. These children seem to have a love affair with life. Think of the gusto with which Betty, or Barbara, or Sam tell even the simplest story about themselves.

Intelligent children act as if they thought the universe made some sense. They check their answers and their thoughts against common sense, while other children, not expecting answers to make sense, not knowing what is sense, see no point in checking, no way of checking. Yet the difference may go deeper than this. It seems as if what we call intelligent children feel that the universe can be trusted even when it does not seem to make any sense, that even when you don't understand it you can be fairly sure that it is not going to play dirty tricks on you. How close this is in spirit to the remark of Einstein's, "I cannot believe that God plays dice with the universe."

On page 54 in the July 1958 *Scientific American*, in the article "Profile of Creativity," there is the following apt comparison:

> The creative scientist analyzes a problem slowly and carefully, then proceeds rapidly with a solution. The less creative man is apt to flounder in disorganized attempts to get a quick answer.

Indeed he is! How often have we seen our answer-grabbers get into trouble. The fact is that problems and answers are simply different ways of looking at a relationship, a structure, an order. A problem is a picture with a piece missing; the answer is the missing piece. The children who take time to see, and feel, and grip the problem, soon find that the answer is there. The ones who get in trouble are the ones who see a problem as an order to start running at top speed from a given starting point, in an unknown direction, to an unknown destination. They dash after the answer before they have considered the problem. What's their big hurry?

Here are Elaine, the answer-grabber, and Barbara, the thinker, at work on the problem $\frac{3}{4} + \frac{2}{5} = ?$

Elaine (adding tops and bottoms, as is her usual custom): Why not $\frac{5}{9}$?

Barbara: $\frac{5}{9}$ is less than $\frac{3}{4}$. She saw that since $\frac{2}{5}$ was added to $\frac{3}{4}$, the answer would have to be bigger than $\frac{3}{4}$; so $\frac{5}{9}$ could not be it. But this went right over Elaine's head.

Elaine: Where's the $\frac{3}{4}$?

Barbara: In the problem!

Yet I doubt that any amount of explaining could have made Elaine understand what Barbara was saying, far less enable her to do the same kind of thinking for herself.

The poor thinker dashes madly after an answer; the good thinker takes his time and looks at the problem. Is the difference merely a matter of a skill in thought, a technique which, with ingenuity and luck, we might teach and train into children? I'm afraid not. The good thinker can take his time because he can tolerate uncertainty, he can stand not knowing. The poor thinker can't stand not knowing; it drives him crazy.

This cannot be completely explained by the fear of being wrong. No doubt this fear puts, say,

Monica under heavy pressure; but Hal is under the same pressure, and maybe I am as well. Monica is not alone in wanting to be right and fearing to be wrong. What is involved here is another insecurity, the insecurity of not having *any* answer to a problem. Monica wants the right answer, yes; but what she wants, first of all, is an answer, any old answer, and she will do almost anything to get some kind of answer. Once she gets it, a large part of the pressure is off. Rachel was like this; so was Gerald, and many others. They can't stand a problem without a solution, even if they know that their solution will probably be wrong. This panicky search for certainty, this inability to tolerate unanswered questions and unsolved problems seems to lie at the heart of many problems of intelligence. But what causes it?

Some might say here that this is all a matter for the psychiatrists. I am not so sure. A person might well be distrustful in personal relationships and still have a kind of intellectual confidence in the universe. Or is this possible? And if so, can it be taught in school?

June 16, 1959

A year ago I was wondering how a child's fears might influence his strategies. This year's work has told me. The strategies of most of these kids have been consistently self-centered, self-protective, aimed above all else at avoiding trouble, embarrassment, punishment, disapproval, or loss of status. This is particularly true of the ones who have had a tough time in school. When they get a problem, I can read their thoughts on their faces, I can almost hear them, "Am I going to get this right? Probably not; what'll happen to me when I get it wrong? Will the teacher get mad? Will the other kids laugh at me? Will my mother and father hear about it? Will they keep me back this year? Why am I so dumb?" And so on.

Even in the room periods, where I did all I could to make the work non-threatening, I was continually amazed and appalled to see the children hedging their bets, covering their losses in advance, trying to fix things so that whatever happened they could feel they had been right, or if wrong, no more wrong than anyone else. "I think it will sort of balance." They are fence-straddlers, afraid ever to commit themselves—and at the age of ten. Playing games like Twenty Questions, which one might have expected them to play for fun, many of them were concerned only to put up a good front, to look as if they knew what they were doing, whether they did or not.

These self-limiting and self-defeating strategies are dictated, above all else, by fear. For many years I have been asking myself why intelligent children act unintelligently at school. The simple answer is, "Because they're scared." I used to suspect that children's defeatism had something to do with their bad work in school, but I thought I could clear it away with hearty cries of "Onward! You can do it!" What I now see for the first time is the mechanism by which fear destroys intelligence, the way it affects a child's whole way of looking at, thinking about, and dealing with life. So we have two problems, not one: to stop children from being afraid, and then to break them of the bad thinking habits into which their fears have driven them.

What is most surprising of all is how much fear there is in school. Why is so little said about it? Perhaps most people do not recognize fear in children when they see it. They can read the grossest signs of fear; they know what the trouble is when a child clings howling to his mother; but the subtler signs of fear escape them. It is these signs, in children's faces, voices, and gestures, in their movements and ways of working, that tell me plainly that most children in school are scared most of the time, many of them very scared. Like good soldiers, they control their fears, live with them, and adjust themselves to them. But the trouble is, and here is a vital difference between school and war, that the adjustments children make to their fears are almost wholly bad, destructive of their intelligence and capacity. The scared fighter may be the best fighter, but the scared learner is always a poor learner.

August 12, 1959

This morning, near the end of the children's concert on the Esplanade, I saw, sitting on my right about forty feet away, what looked like a retarded child. Beside her sat her very attractive, suburban-looking mother, and another woman. The child looked about thirteen, though it was hard to tell. She was eating a sandwich, and drinking milk through a straw out of a half-pint carton. Every so often she slowly, deliberately brought the sandwich up to her mouth, took a bite, and chewed it as she lowered the sandwich to her lap. Then she carefully raised the carton, centered the straw exactly, and took a careful sip. One might have thought the carton contained nitroglycerine from her way of handling it. Frequently, she looked briefly and silently at her mother, who was conversing with the other woman and seemed to be paying no attention to her. I realized later that she was looking to see whether what she was doing was all right.

What first struck me about this child, as so often is the case with seriously retarded children, was the extraordinary ugliness of her face. Yet there was nothing especially wrong with her features, except a kind of sick down-turning of the mouth. She could never have been called pretty, but her features were normal and regular, and her coloring normal, though a bit pale and unhealthy looking.

My shock, horror, and pity for her and her mother, were so strong as to block any thinking. I concentrated on watching without seeming to watch. She was so intent on her milk and sandwich that she did not notice me. And as I watched an interesting thing happened. The orchestra, which was playing a piece that almost surely she did not know, reached the closing bars, and as it did the girl put down her food, looked toward the orchestra, and raised her hands as if ready to clap. A moment later the piece ended, and hearing others clap, she began to clap.

The concert over, the conductor began to say the usual words, "We're glad you've come. Come again next year, etc.," and the girl, without changing the ghastly expression on her face, raised her arm stiffly in what I realized after a while was a gesture of good-bye. She seemed to be going through a ritual. When people are leaving, you wave good-bye. This orchestra was leaving, so she waved good-bye; but not because she was communicating something to the orchestra, only because it was something that she had been trained to do.

As the mother and friend continued to eat and chat, I moved to the shade of a tree, where I could watch unobtrusively. Into my mind there came a conversation I had recently had with a close friend, about the rightness or wrongness of killing deformed children in infancy. He had said that he had always thought he might leave a deformed baby with its face in a pillow, so that its death might look like an accident. I asked whether he thought a wife would ever agree to this, and we agreed that it is something a mother would probably never do. At the same time, he felt that to keep such children alive was so terrible for both mother and child that it would be better for the child to be dead.

This conversation, boiling up in my mind, crowded out any thinking about the retarded girl; but after a while I began to think about her again. Why was she so terrible to look at? What is so horrifying about mentally defective children in general? Is it the contrast between what we think of as human qualities and the lack of these qualities in someone of human shape? My mind made a sentence, as if talking to someone: "We have to see someone who is less than human to appreciate what it means to be human."

But then, I thought, there is nothing horrifying about the less than human, about animals, for instance. I suddenly realized that what made this child horrifying to see would have been equally horrifying in an animal. Have you ever seen a dog perpetually scared out of his wits, tail curled between his legs, always looking over his shoulder, slinking around, shying and leaping at every noise? That, too, is horrifying. What made this child terrible to see was not that she was less than fully human, but that she was less than fully animal.

When we say a child is retarded, what do we mean? Why, that she is mentally and emotionally like much younger children. Yet only a look at the younger children on the grass, listening, fooling around, dreaming, playing, teasing, was enough to show that this poor child, though perhaps mentally six or seven years old, was like no six-year-old, or three-year-old, who ever lived.

About this time mother and friend got up, folded their blanket, and started to walk across the grass in the opposite direction. As they passed the now empty bandshell, the girl again raised her arm in another stiff wave—and then her mother gently reached up and drew her hand down again, and, lest the child think this a rebuke, held her hand as they walked the rest of the way across the grass. It seemed to me that she brought the girl's hand down because to wave at an empty bandshell was inappropriate, the kind of thing a much younger child might do, might even be petted and admired for.

Let us say that retarded children are children who, for one reason or another, are slower to learn the ropes, to pick up what their elders think is appropriate behavior for their age. What must their home life be like? I have a mental picture of the life of this child; I see her, hundreds and thousands of times, doing something which is not bad, not wrong, but just inappropriate for her age, and being told, gently or sorrowfully, not to do it. What a confusion in her mind! It is hard enough for children to learn to do and not to do the things that are really necessary—don't touch, don't run into the street, don't go in the medicine cabinet, etc. If we add to this already long list all the things that a retarded child would be told not to do "because you're too old for that," it is easy to see how such a child's reasoning power and faith in the world could break down altogether.

My point is not that retarded children are made, not born. No; I daresay this child really was retarded. What puzzles me is, if I.Q. measures even roughly the rate at which we learn, why a child with an I.Q. of 50 should not *in time* get to be a reasonably normal and competent person. It is said that, in terms of what he knows and can figure out, the average adult is not much beyond the level of the average twelve-year-old. For all my skepticism about the measurement and testing of intelligence, I think this reflects some kind of truth. Then why should not the child with the I.Q. of 50 catch up with the crowd, more or less, by the time he is twenty-five? What happens to him along the way to ensure that he will never catch up? What turned this particular child from a girl whose body was too big for her behavior into a kind of monster of fear and tension that would make you sick at heart to watch?

I thought that had she been acting like a normal, healthy child of half her age, she would have been less distressing to watch. Then my mind's eye conjured up a picture of her, romping around at the concert like a six-year-old, and I sensed very vividly the horror that this inappropriate behavior would arouse in all who saw it. So it may well be that the tension we see in retarded children is caused, not so much by their being prevented from doing things that to them seem perfectly natural, as by the horror and revulsion that their inappropriate behavior arouses in all who see it, including, and perhaps above all, their own parents. For we may be sure that, retarded or not, they sense and understand these feelings, which are vastly more effective and terrible than any punishment.

A great deal of the training of retarded children must be aimed at concealing their condition, at making them look as if they were brighter than they are. The child who is mentally six is obliged to play the role of a child of twelve. Like the child this morning, whose entire attention was concentrated on *not spilling* (who would care if a six-year-old spilled something?), they have to think self-consciously about every single thing they do. They must lead lives something like the heroes of stories of impersonation, who, pretending to be someone else, must continually remember to walk, talk, whistle, sing, scratch, move a certain way, *always*, with detection, capture, and death the penalty for forgetting. The task must be enough to break the spirit of all but the most practiced, disciplined, and self-confident adult. Small wonder that it should be far too much for a child who is untrained, fearful, and all too aware of the low opinion most people have of him. Even the impersonator, the spy, gets a rest now and then; the mentally six-year-old trying to act twelve hardly ever does. The picture is almost too nightmarish to think about. Perhaps I exaggerate; but then, remembering the face of this child, I think not. It would take a living nightmare to make that kind of haunted face.

If adult intolerance of behavior that to these kids seems natural makes terrified monsters out of what began as merely slow children, what are we to do? We have to draw some line between behavior approved and disapproved, or how is the child to learn? But the great difference between the normal child and the retarded child is that the former is punished for his "bad" behavior; the latter may not be punished, but he is abhorred, which is far worse.

Is it possible that such exaggerated adult reactions to children's misbehavior may tend to make juvenile delinquents? The other day I was walking across Boston Common when I saw two boys having a spitting contest. This in itself would fall far outside the bounds of what most adults would consider tolerable. Why are we so sensitive to spitting? It didn't bother me that much, so I walked closer to see who was winning and to get the reactions of other passers-by. Then the smaller boy began to do something that overshot my bounds of the tolerable. He began to spit at the other boy. He wasn't a very good shot, and didn't hit him; but it upset me. I was further upset by his voice, which was loud, harsh, hoarse, gravelly, with the hysterical overtones of someone always on the edge of a fight. Then they noticed me watching, and with one voice started saying, "Hey mister, gimme a nickel to ride home, etc." I wanted no more to do with them, and walked away. I regret the reaction, but in the same case I would probably react that way again.

There must be children, and this small boy might well be one of them, who, being of stronger character than our poor retarded girl, react differently to the shock and horror which their behavior rouses in adults. Far from making themselves sick with anxiety trying to avoid rousing this horror in adults, these kids look for ways to rouse it. They recognize that their ability to shock and horrify is a kind of power over other people.

If strong disapproval of children's behavior makes neurotics at one end and terrorists at the other, what should we do? Perhaps the answer is to give both kinds of children things to use their human powers on that will be more interesting than either their fears or the possibility of arousing fear in others. Not that this will be easy to do; but it is where we should aim.

October 3, 1959

Yesterday, three young boys were riding the subway to Park Street. They were exceedingly noisy, excited, and rude. They may not have been "delinquents," but they looked as if they could have been, and certainly as if they wanted the rest of us to think they were. The sudden contact with them was shocking. They seemed so far from what we are used to in people, so close to wild animals—but that is a libel on animals. It was hard not to feel that there was no open door through which they could be reached. About them in the car was an aura of stiff and anxious resentment, which they seemed to recognize and enjoy. People were mentally drawing their skirts and coattails aside.

As I watched these boys, I began to see them as they were. Each time one of them said or did something to shock the people in the car, he looked quickly and anxiously at the faces of his companions, to see whether he had won their approval. Then it would be the turn of another to try to outdo him in noisiness and rowdiness, and to look for his approval in turn. It was suddenly clear that these boys were alone, anxious, frightened, and ready to do anything, anything at all, that would, if only for a moment, gain them the approval of their fellows. For their security they had nothing but each other, and they were so anxious that they had almost no security to give. Every time one of them laughed at another's joke, his laughter was almost instantly cut short by the need to do something that would make the other laugh at him. Their approval of each other almost instantly soured into jealousy.

What did these boys have to nourish their self-respect and self-esteem besides the short-lived and uneasy approval they gave each other? Only the palpable disapproval of everyone else around them, a disapproval close to fear. If you can't make people like you, it is something to be able to make them afraid of you.

Harrison Salisbury, in *The Shook-Up Generation*, and Warren Miller, in *The Cool World*, describe, the former as reporter, the latter as novelist, the world of the delinquent. It appears from what they say that even in the most tightly knit street gangs there is little of what we would call friendship. Gang members are no more than uneasy allies, welded together partly by fear of the world outside and partly by the certain knowledge that nobody else in the world gives a damn about them.

December 14, 1959

It often seemed last year as if Garry was deliberately turning back from the world of success, which was strange to him, and which, though it offered new and sweet rewards, might also contain hidden dangers, in favor of the world of failure in which, even if he was not very happy, he was at least at home. Today I saw, more clearly than ever before, why failure, unrelieved and total, may seem to some students to be a promising strategy for school and even for life.

Trudy is bright, has a keen sense of the ridiculous, and is more or less the class screwball. Her schoolwork is very poor, by any standards, her spelling perhaps worst of all. On her papers she spells worse than an average third-grader. During the first part of the fall her spelling did not improve at all. Finally, after many struggles and failures—everything I learn about teaching I learn from the bad students—I have come up with some ideas that seem to help, even with the poor spellers.

When a child misspells a word on a paper, I print the word correctly with Magic Marker on a 3 x 5 card. The children use these like a tachistoscope. By moving a blank card quickly over the printed card, I give them a split second look at the word, then ask them to spell it. They can have as many looks as they want; but each one is very short. This prevents them from spelling the word aloud in their heads, and then trying to remember what they "said." I want them to use their eye to see what a word looks like, and their mind's eye to remember what it looks like.

The bad spellers, of course, accumulate quite a stack of cards. I tell them that if they spell one of these words correctly on a surprise test, I will remove it from their cards. They all enjoy reducing their piles of spelling cards, which seem to hang over their heads a little. Today I gave Trudy a surprise test. It was a surprise for me; she got about twenty words right out of twenty-five. What surprised me most of all, when she had finished this good performance, was to see her looking, not pleased or satisfied, but anxious. I thought, "Becoming a better speller presents risks to this child. What on earth can they be?" And then I saw why for some children the strategy of weakness, of incompetence, of impotence, may be a good one. For, after all, if *they* (meaning we) know that you can't do anything, *they* won't expect you to do anything, and *they* won't blame you or punish you for not being able to do what you have been told to do. I could almost hear the girl saying plaintively to herself, "I suppose he's going to expect me to spell right all the time now, and he'll probably give me heck when I don't."

Children who depend heavily on adult approval may decide that, if they can't have total success, their next-best bet is to have total failure. Perhaps, in using the giving or withholding of approval as a way of making children do what we want, we are helping to make these deliberate failers. I think of a sixteen-year-old boy I once knew who, unable to fulfill all his father's very high expectations for him, decided to fulfill none of them. The father was a pillar of the community, good at everything he did; the boy became a playboy and a drunk. One night, at a party, the father was watching his son doing a very drunken and quite funny tango alone in the middle of the dance floor, before a laughing and admiring crowd. The thought flashed through my mind, "Well, that's one thing he can do better than you can."

It is often said that alcoholics may be very able people who feel they cannot meet the high standards they have set for themselves, and hence don't try. Perhaps children find, or try to find, in hopeless incompetence the kind of refuge that an alcoholic finds in liquor. But how do we get children to kick the failure habit? Do we organize a society of Failers Anonymous?

Incompetence has one other advantage. Not only does it reduce what others expect and demand of you, it reduces what you expect or even hope for yourself. When you set out to fail, one thing is certain—you can't be disappointed. As the old saying goes, you can't fall out of bed when you sleep on the floor.

January 3, 1960

Some people say that it is bad to read old-fashioned fairy tales to little children, because they make them afraid. But even without fairy tales, the lives of little children are full of fears. Like very primitive people, they live in a world that they cannot begin to understand. Fairy tales could do for small children, and indeed did for many years, what myth, ritual, and religion did for primitive peoples—give their fears a name and an identity, a handle to take hold of and perhaps to cast them out by. A child who can channel his fear of the unknown into a fear of ghosts, witches, ogres, giants, wicked fairies, and the like, may be able to rid himself of much of that fear when he finds that such things do not exist. Even if not, he will have had practice in dealing with fear, in facing and thinking about what he is afraid of.

A small boy I knew, when he was about four, used to tell to any sympathetic listener endless stories about his particular monster, which he called a Mountain-Lion-Eater. I suppose he had begun with stories about a mountain lion, that being the fiercest thing he could think of, and had later learned enough about real mountain lions to feel that they were not large or terrible enough to contain all the fear and terror that he wanted to put into them. But something that ate mountain lions!—that might just fill the bill. And this was no ordinary monster. He ate up, not only mountain lions, but houses, neighborhoods, cities, even the whole world, when he was in the mood. In some stories, the little boy overcame the monster; in others, the monster ate him up. It all depended on how he felt at the moment. In either case, his private mythology did him a great service by enabling him in part to see from outside and acknowledge his courage or his fear.

July 20, 1960   *on babies*

My seventeen-month-old niece caught sight of my ball point pen the other day, and reached out for it. It has a plastic cap that fits over the point. She took hold of it, and after some pushing and pulling, got the cap off. After looking it over, she put it back on. Then off again; then on again. A good game! Now, if I want to be able to use my pen, I have to keep it out of sight, for when she sees it, she wants to play with it. She is so deft in putting it back on that it makes me wonder about all I've read about the lack of coordination in infants and the imprecision of their movements. Under the right circumstances—when they are interested—they may be much more skillful than we think.

These quiet summer days I spend many hours watching this baby. What comes across most vividly is that she is a kind of scientist. She is always observing and experimenting. She is hardly ever idle. Most of her waking time she is intensely and purposefully active, soaking up experience and trying to make sense out of it, trying to find how things around her behave, and trying to make them behave as she wants them to.

In the face of what looks like unbroken failure, she is so persistent. Most of her experiments, her efforts to predict and control her environment, don't work. But she goes right on, not the least daunted. Perhaps this is because there are no penalties attached to failure, except nature's— ʾally, if you try to step on a ball, you fall down.

A baby does not react to failure as an adult does, or even a five-year-old, because she has not yet been made to feel that failure is shame, disgrace, a crime. Unlike her elders, she is not concerned with protecting herself against everything that is not easy and familiar; she reaches out to experience, she embraces life.

Watching this baby, it is hard to credit the popular notion that without outside rewards and penalties children will not learn. There are some rewards and penalties in her life; the adults approve of some things she does, and disapprove of others. But most of the time she lives beyond praise or blame, if only because most of her learning experiments are unobserved. After all, who thinks about the meaning of what a baby is doing, so long as she is quiet and contented? But watch a while and think about it, and you see that she has a strong desire to make sense of the world around her. Her learning gives her great satisfaction, whether anyone else notices it or not.

February 26, 1961

The unbelievable incompetence of some of the kids sometimes drives me wild. They can't find anything. They have no paper or pencil when it's time for work. Their desks are a mess. They lose library books. If they do homework at home, they leave it there; if they take home material to do homework, they leave the assignment at school. They can't keep their papers in a notebook. Yet they are not stupid or incapable children; they do many things well.

Ted is a very intelligent, alert, curious, humorous, and attractive boy, with a record of unbroken failure and frustration in school. He is an excellent athlete, strong, quick, and well coordinated. But his school papers are as torn, smudged, rumpled, and illegible as any I have ever seen. The other day the class was cleaning out desks, and I was "helping" him. We got about a ream of loose papers out of the desk, and I asked him to put them in the notebook. As always, when he is under tension, his face began to get red. He squirmed and fidgeted, and began to mutter, "They won't fit, the notebook's the wrong size,"—which wasn't true. Finally he assembled a thick stack of papers and began to try to jam them onto one of the rings in his notebook, not noticing that the holes in the papers were at least a half-inch from the ring. As he pushed and fumbled and muttered, I felt my blood pressure rising until, exasperated almost to rage, I said loudly, "For Heaven's sake, leave it alone, do it later, I can't stand to watch any more of it!"

Thinking over this scene, and many others like it, I was suddenly reminded of a movie, *A Walk in the Sun,* based on the novel by Harry Brown. It showed the adventures of a leaderless platoon of infantrymen during the first day of the invasion of Italy. At one point, while the platoon is moving through some woods, they are surprised by an enemy light tank, which, amid a good deal of confusion, they manage to ambush. When this action is over the soldiers find that their sergeant, who has been growing rapidly more anxious, and is clearly the victim of battle fatigue, has given way completely. They find him hugging the ground, shaking all over, babbling incoherently. They leave him behind, as they move inland toward their vaguely conceived objective. One of the soldiers remarks as they go that the sergeant has finally dug himself a foxhole that they can't get him out of.

It seems to me that children dig themselves similar foxholes in school, that their fumbling incompetence is in many ways comparable to the psychoneurotic reactions of men who have been under too great a stress for too long. Many will reject this comparison as being wildly exaggerated and inappropriate. They are mistaken. There are very few children who do not feel, during most of the time they are in school, an amount of fear, anxiety, and tension that most adults would find intolerable. It is no coincidence at all that in many of their worst nightmares adults find themselves back in school. I was a successful student, yet now and then I have such nightmares myself. In mine I am always going to a class from which, without the slightest excuse, I have been absent for months. I know that I am hopelessly behind in the work, and that my long absence is going to get me in serious trouble, of what sort I am not sure. Yet I feel I cannot stay away any longer, I have to go.

It is bad enough to be a teacher and feel that the children in your charge are using the conscious and controlled parts of their minds in ways which, in the long run and even in the short, are unprofitable, limiting, and self-defeating; to see them dutifully doing the assigned work and to be sure that they are not getting a scrap of intellectual nourishment out of it; to know that what they seem to have learned today they will have forgotten by next month, or next week, or even tomorrow.

But it is a good deal worse to feel that many children are reacting to school in ways that are not under their control at all. To feel that you are helping make children less intelligent is bad enough, without having to wonder whether you may be helping to make them neurotic as well.

March 2, 1961

A woman who has spent many years working with children with severe learning blocks, children whom conventional schools, even in slow sections, could not deal with at all, told a class of teachers the other day that early investigators of children who could not read coined the term "word-blindness" to describe what they saw. There has been much talk about "word-blindness" since. The experts of the moment seem to believe that the cause is neurological, that there is in a certain percentage of children something in the organization and structure of the brain which makes word recognition difficult or impossible.

Perhaps this is the cause of some reading problems, but that it is the only or the most frequent cause is open to grave doubt. My own belief is that blindness to patterns or symbols, such as words, is in most instances emotional and psychological, rather than neurological. It is a neurotic reaction to too great stress. I have often experienced it myself.

The most severe case came during a flute lesson. I describe it in some detail because the kind of tensions that are needed to bring about this loss of the ability to see meaningfully are such that, except in time of war or extreme danger, most adults are not likely to experience them.

The lesson was in the late afternoon. I had had a difficult and discouraging day in class, followed by a tense and unpleasant committee meeting. I was late in leaving, was delayed by heavy traffic, and arrived late for my lesson, with no chance to warm up. My teacher had also had a trying day, and was not his usual patient self. He was exasperated that I had made so little progress since the previous lesson, and began, as exasperated teachers do, to try by brute will power to force me to play the assigned passage as fast as he thought I should be able to play it.

The pace was much too fast; I began to make mistakes; I wanted to stop, but, cowed by his determination, hesitated to make the suggestion. A feeling of physical pressure built up in my head. It felt as if something inside were trying to burst it open, but also as if something outside were pressing it in. Some kind of noise, other than my miserable playing, was in my ears. Suddenly I became totally noteblind. The written music before me lost all meaning. *All* meaning. It is hard to describe what I felt. It lasted no more than a second or two, only as long as it took me to stop playing and look away from the music. I could see the notes, but it was as if I could not see them. It is said of such moments that everything becomes a blur. This may have been true; when to go on seeing clearly becomes unbearably painful, the eyes may well refuse to focus. There was also an impression that the notes were moving and shifting on the page. But above all else was the impression that, whatever I was seeing, it was as if I had never seen such things before, never heard of them, never imagined them. Any and all associations they might have had for me were, for that instant, destroyed. They were completely disconnected from all my previous experience.[1]

These sensations were indescribably frightening and unpleasant. After a second or two, I put down my flute and turned away from the music. My teacher sensed that I had been driven over the edge of something, and after a short rest, we went on at a more relaxed pace. But suppose I had been a child? Suppose I had not been free, or felt free, to turn away? Suppose my teacher had felt that it would be good for my character to force the pace harder than ever?

March 5, 1961

Some people say of non-readers, "These children can't or don't read because of the way they use their minds." Others retort, "No; they don't read because of the kind of minds they have." The argument seems to me unreal as well as useless. The distinction between what our minds are and how we use them is one that exists only for purposes of talk; it does not exist at the level of reality. The mind is not a kind of thinking machine that someone or something inside of us uses, well or badly. It *is*; and it works, perhaps well, perhaps badly; and the way it works one time has much to do with the way it will work another time.

---

[1] A friend told me not long ago that, during a recent music lesson, she had exactly the same experience.

Religious mystics in India, so we are told, stand for many years with an arm raised, or a limb distorted or immobilized in some fashion. After a while the limb becomes unusable. What sense does it make to argue whether the cause of this is physical, or lies in the way the limb was used? It was the way it was used that made it the kind of limb it was, a limb that could not be used any other way. It is probably true of the mind, as well, that the way we use it determines how we can use it. If we use it badly long enough, it will become less and less possible to use it well. If we use it well, the possibility grows that we may use it even better. We must be wary, then, of assuming that because some learning difficulties seem to be caused by brain disfunction they are therefore incurable. The brain, as an organ, may have far more flexibility and recuperative powers than we realize. What it cannot accomplish one way it may be able to do another. Conversely, we must be aware of the extent to which, in causing children to make poor use of their minds, we may be making their minds less and less useful to them.

March 21, 1961

Today Andy had a long, tough session with me. He finally solved the problem I had given him. But I can't help wondering what he learned. Not much; he certainly didn't gain any insight into the property of multiplication in which I was interested. All that he had to show for his time was the memory of a long and painful experience, full of failure, frustration, anxiety, and tension. He did not even feel satisfaction when he had done the problem correctly, only relief at not having to think about it any more.

He is not stupid. In spite of his nervousness and anxiety, he is curious about some things, bright, enthusiastic, perceptive, and in his writing highly imaginative. But he is, literally, scared out of his wits. He cannot learn math because his mind moves so slowly from one thought to another that the connections between them are lost. His memory does not hold what he learns, above all else because he won't trust it. Every day he must figure out, all over again, that $9 + 7 = 16$, because how can he be sure that it has not changed, or that he has not made another in an endless series of mistakes? How can you trust any of your own thoughts when so many of them have proved to be wrong?

I can see no kind of life for him unless he can break out of the circle of failure, discouragement, and fear in which he is trapped. But I can't see how he is going to break out. Worst of all, I'm not sure that we, his elders, really want him to break out. It is no accident that this boy is afraid. We have made him afraid, consciously, deliberately, so that we might more easily control his behavior and get him to do whatever we wanted him to do.

I am horrified to realize how much I myself use fear and anxiety as instruments of control. I think, or at least hope, that the kids in my class are somewhat more free of fear than they have been in previous classes, or than most children are in most classes. I try to use a minimum of controls and pressures. Still, the work must be done—mustn't it?—and there must be some limits to what they can be allowed to do in class, and the methods I use for getting the work done and controlling the behavior rest ultimately on fear, fear of getting in wrong with me, or the school, or their parents.

Here is Andy, whose fears make him almost incapable of most kinds of constructive thinking and working. On the one hand, I try to dissipate those fears. But on the other, I have to do something to get him to do the work he so hates doing. What I do boils down to a series of penalties, which are effective in exactly the proportion that they rouse the kind of fears that I have been trying to dispel. Also, when children feel a little relieved of the yoke of anxiety that they are so used to bearing, they behave just like other people freed from yokes, like prisoners released, like victors in a revolution, like small-town businessmen on American Legion conventions. They cut up; they get bold and sassy; they may for a while try to give a hard time to those adults who for so long have been giving them a hard time. So, to keep him in his place, to please the school and his parents, I have to make him fearful again. The freedom from fear that I try to give with one hand I almost instantly take away with the other.

What sense does this make?

REAL LEARNING

April 22, 1958

We tell children here to think about the meaning of what they are doing. We say this is the sure way to the right answer. But it may lead instead into one of the paradoxes and contradictions of which elementary math is full. In such cases the student who thinks, as I used to, "Oh well, I'll just do what they tell me, and not worry about it," can often move on without difficulty, while the one who thinks hard about what he is doing can get into a tangle from which neither he nor his teachers may be able to free him.

One of the fifth-grade groups was trying to discover how to divide by fractions. They had been given, to figure out for themselves if they could, "Divide 6 by ½." The children know the official school definition of division, that "8 divided by 4" means either "How many 4's are contained in 8?" or "If you separate 8 into 4 equal parts, how many will be in each part?" Most of the group applied the first meaning of division to the problem, taking it to mean, "How many ½'s are contained in 6?"

They saw that the answer was 12. But two girls, who had done excellent thinking about multiplying fractions only a few days before, tried to apply the other meaning of division, and asked themselves: "If you divide 6 into halves, how big will each half be?" Quite reasonably, they got the answer 3.

It was their good thinking, and my bad, that got them into difficulty. I had not told them that the second of the two meanings of division did not apply, and was in fact without meaning in the case of division by a fraction. The reason I had not told them is that I had not realized it myself. Since I had given them the rule, they felt that it must make sense, and in fact twisted it to make sense in the only way it could be made to make sense. Six divided into half a part could only mean six divided into halves.

My misuse of language reinforced their misunderstanding. Like most people, I frequently use the word "divide" in a way that contradicts its mathematical meaning. We say: "Divide a pie into four parts" when all we are really doing is making two perpendicular cuts through the center of the pie; we say, "Divide a line into two parts," when what we mean is to find the mid-point of the line; we talk about dividing something in half when it would be more consistent to talk about dividing it in two. For all these reasons it was natural for these girls to suppose that dividing 6 by ½ meant dividing it into halves, or two parts.

One able boy unwittingly increased their confusion. Early in the period he explained at the blackboard that the problem was asking how many ½'s were contained in 6, and showed with a good diagram that the answer was 12. Then he made a mistake that many adults might easily have made. He said, "Twelve what?" Then, after a second's thought, he answered, "Twelve halves," and wrote $1\frac{2}{2}$ on the board. He soon saw his mistake, and corrected it; but too late to save the girls. They had seen a leading member of the opposition go to the board, and using the other meaning of division, prove that 6 divided by $\frac{1}{2}$ is $1\frac{2}{2}$, or 6. Since this was nonsense, they were all the more convinced that their own answer was right.

Other children began to try to show the girls where they had gone wrong, but without success. To rescue a man lost in the woods, you must get to where he is. The other children could not get to where these girls were, could not see how they had arrived at their answer, and hence could not help them. All they could do, like most teachers, was repeat over and over again how they got their own answer—which was no help at all. One boy asked one of the girls to work out $6 \times \frac{1}{2}$ on the board. She wrote, "$6 \times \frac{1}{2} = 3$." He then pointed out that they had just said that 6 *divided* by $\frac{1}{2}$ equaled 3. The girl looked at her partner and said, "We've been tricked!" I wonder how often we, their teachers, make them feel this way.

Here one girl began to feel that the answer 3 was somehow wrong, and whispered to her partner, "We goofed." Later she said, "$\frac{1}{2}$ of 6 is the same as multiplication." She still could not see clearly that what she was doing was multiplying, not dividing. Finally, after much further argument, she said to her partner, "We may as well give in. Half of 6 is 12. I don't get it, but it is."

These words threw a sharp light on the world of school as seen through the eyes of children.

How much of my teaching has been accepted by the children in just this spirit? What I tell a child may seem to contradict his common sense, the common usage of English, and even other things I have told him; but he must bow to superior force and accept it whether it makes sense or not.

I was finally able to get the girls out of their jam, and admitted my own responsibility for getting them into it. But I had been thinking and talking for some weeks about possible contradictions in my own teaching, and so was particularly sensitive to it. This incident shows that we teachers must begin to try to look at our ideas and our teaching through the eyes of someone who knows nothing, can accept nothing unproven, and cannot tolerate inconsistency and paradox. We must try to free our teaching from ambiguity, confusion, and self-contradiction. Since to bring clarity and consistency to "elementary" mathematics is one of the central mathematical problems of our time, this task will not be easy.

July 28, 1958

One day, some years ago, some friends said, "Ever seen any silicone putty?" I said I had never even heard of it. They gave me a lump. I kneaded it, flattened it, stretched it into a long thin piece, tore it into smaller pieces. Then they said, "Roll it into a ball, and throw it on the floor." I did so. My eye, and my brain, and my very bones knew what would happen—the putty would splat on the floor and stick. I threw it, and while my eye, so to speak, stayed stuck to the floor the putty bounced up as high as my head. For an awful split second, the universe rocked around me. I was on the brink of terror. Then, in this same instant, something wrenched in my mind, something said, "OK, so it bounces, very funny, what'll they think of next?" and I was back in the world of order and reason.

This makes me think of the little girl—first grader? second grader?—who burst into tears the other day when her teacher told the class how to spell "once." The teacher probably assumed that the child cried because the word was so hard. The chances are that she cried because the word was so crazy, because it smashed into pieces the understanding that she had been carefully building up in her mind about the way words are spelled. Even then, she could probably have lived with this crazy word if only the teacher had troubled to point out that it was crazy. What really makes school hard for *thinkers* is not just that teachers say so much that doesn't make sense, but that they say it in exactly the way they say things that are sensible, so that the child comes to feel—as he is intended to—that when he doesn't understand it is his fault.

What seems simple, natural, and self-evident to us may not seem so to a child. Take, for example, the numeral 10. We are so used to it that we cannot imagine what it might be like, knowing what 1 and 0 stand for, to be told that when you put them together it stands for something much bigger than either of them. We should acknowledge the obvious *nuttiness* of this when we first present this numeral to children, so that they will not feel on the outside of a baffling mystery. Otherwise this first encounter with 10 may give children a shock from which they never fully recover, and which freezes up their minds every time they think about it.

November 13, 1958

Kids have trouble with arithmetic, not only because they have to memorize a host of facts that seem to have no pattern, meaning, or interest, but also because they are given a host of rules for manipulating these facts, which they have to take on faith. I don't continually have to check my arithmetic operations against the world of numbers, because I have proved to my satisfaction that the rules for manipulating numerals have their roots in the world of real quantities and really work there. I know I can safely use the conventional method to multiply 24×36 because I know that this means the same thing as $(20 \times 30) + (4 \times 30) + (20 \times 6) + (4 \times 6)$. But if I didn't know that this was true, what sense would the conventional system of multiplication make? How could I feel that this mysterious business of "bringing down the zero" and "moving the next line over" would give me the right answer? How could I ever check it against reality and common sense?

The beauty of the Cuisenaire rods [1] is not only

[1] Since I will be describing the work of children with the Cuisenaire rods, a word about them is in order. Named after their inventor, a Belgian schoolteacher, they are a set of wooden rods, or sticks, one centimeter (cm.) wide and one cm. high, about the thickness of one's little finger; they vary in length from 1 cm. to 10 cm. (1 cm. = about ⅜″). Each length of rod is painted its own color: 1 cm.—white; 2 cm.—red; 3 cm.—light

that they enable the child to discover, by himself, how to carry out certain operations, but also that they enable him to satisfy himself that these operations really work, really describe what happens.

November 26, 1958

Do the Cuisenaire rods give us as much control over bad strategy as we like to think? Is there not a chance that some of the strategists may not still be slipping something over on us? I imagine a student, like our old friend Emily. I say, "What is the 3 of the 4?" *"Three-fourths."* "What is the four of the three?" *"Four-thirds."* "What is the 4 of the 5?" *"Four-fifths."* "What is the 5 of the 4?" *"Five-fourths."* Sure, I ask children to look at the rods as they do this. But do the rods themselves determine the answer? Might not the students be

---

green; 4 cm.—crimson (often called "pink" by the children); 5 cm.—yellow; 6 cm.—dark green; 7 cm.—black; 8 cm.—brown; 9 cm.—blue; 10 cm.—orange.

In writing about the use of the rods, I will often call them by their colors; but I will put their length in centimeters as a reminder, thus: yellow (5).

Anyone particularly interested in children's work with arithmetic would probably do well to get a set of the rods, so that they may use them to see for themselves what some of the children I describe were actually doing. For information about the rods, write the Cuisenaire Corp. of America, 9 Elm Avenue, Mt. Vernon, N.Y.

Though the rods were invented and first used by Cuisenaire, their use has been greatly expanded and refined by Dr. C. Gattegno, a British professor of mathematics and psychology, who introduced them into many other countries, including the United States, where they are used (and misused) in a rapidly increasing number of schools.

playing a word-shoving game with us? Suppose I said to Emily, "What is the blip of the blop?" Might she not answer, "*Blip blopths.*" "What is the blop of the blip?" "*Blop blipths.*" Isn't this a perfectly good strategy? It gives right answers. I suspect that Caroline and Monica are doing just this, and I heard Gil say the other day something about, "You take the one that comes first . . ." Merely telling them to hold onto the rods and look at them will not frustrate this strategy.

One way of dealing with these strategists is to vary the form of our questions. We might hold up a yellow (5) rod, and say, "If this is 1, show me ⅗"; or, "If this is 2, show me 4." Such questions might test more fully whether they were really seeing the rods and their relationships.

Isn't there something to be said for asking, whenever possible, questions that can be answered without words? Questions that can be answered by doing something, showing us something?

December 6, 1958

OBSERVING IN BILL HULL'S CLASS:

The other day you were doing that business with the kids in which you hold up two rods and ask what one is of the other. I noticed after a while that you always asked, first, what the small one was of the large. The children answered with a fraction in which the smaller number was the numerator. I noticed then that if you paused, or looked doubtful, or repeated the question, some of them quickly reversed their answer. If they had said five-sevenths, they then said seven-fifths. Three people did this; Rachel, one of the boys, and Barbara.

It was Barbara who really made the dent on me, because she is usually such a thoughtful and capable student. You held up the black (7) and the blue (9), and, reversing your previous procedure, said, "What is the blue of the black?" She said, "Seven-ninths." You hesitated. Her face got red, she stared at you, not at the rods, for a second and then said, "Nine-sevenths." Nothing in her face, voice, or manner gave me the feeling that she had the slightest idea why the first answer was wrong and the second right, or even that she was sure that the second was right. If *she* is not sure, I don't like to think about the others.

We want the rods to turn the mumbo-jumbo of arithmetic into sense. The danger is that the mumbo-jumbo may engulf the rods instead. It doesn't do any good to tell Monica to look at the rods if she doesn't believe that when she looks she will find the answer there. She will only have two mysteries to contend with instead of one.

December 7, 1958

One day in math class I was trying to make the point that division is not just a trick that we carry out with numerals, but an operation that could be done even by someone who didn't know any numerals. I asked them to suppose that they had a large bag of marbles, which they wanted to divide as evenly as possible among four people, and furthermore, that they had no way of counting them. Most of the children realized that by giving out a marble at a time to each person in turn until all the marbles were gone, they could do the job. But Pat and one other kid had a different idea. Here is Pat's paper.

> You could measure the bag with a ruler, and say it measures to be 8 so then you would measure 2 inches of the bag for each one because there are four people and 2×4 is 8 so you measure four 2 inch marks and then you could cut on each 2 inch line like this [small picture here of a bag of marbles with four lines going down it, evenly spaced] and give each person as much as from one 2 inch line to another.

The other one said the same thing in different words. One at a time, I spoke to them. To each I said, "Imagine that I have a big bag of marbles in my hand," (business of showing, by gestures, what a large, heavy bag of marbles would look and feel like). Then I said, "Now in this other hand I have some scissors," (Imitation of scissors). "Now I hold the bag in this hand, and I bring the scissors over, and I start cutting this bag in half (gesturing of cutting); what is going to happen?" At this point Pat said "Oh!"; the other child laughed. Then they both said that the marbles would go all over the floor. Only then did they realize that their answer to the problem of dividing up the marbles didn't make any sense.

This brings to mind something that happened when I was in prep school. A friend was studying for a chemistry test. He was trying to memorize which of a list of salts were soluble in water. Going through the list, he said that calcium carbonate was soluble. I asked him to name some common materials made of calcium carbonate. He named limestone, granite, and marble. I asked, "Do you often see these things dissolving in the rain?" He had never thought of that. Between what he was studying for chemistry and the real world, the world of his senses and common sense, there was no connection.

February 6, 1959

I have a hunch. Suppose we ask the children to draw two lines, one of them $5/7$ of the other. They will probably draw a 5-inch and a 7-inch line. But then suppose we ask them to draw two more lines, one of them $5/17$ of the other. I wonder how many of them will come up after a while and say it can't be done, because they can't get a 17-inch line on their paper.[1]

Perhaps we can say of understanding that the better we understand something, the more places we can use it. If so, then one way to get children to understand fractions may be to think of as many ways as possible to have them use fractions.

I feel myself beginning to understand the difference between fractions as quantities and fractions as operators. The expression $1/2 + 1/3 = 5/6$ can mean that $1/2$ of 1, plus $1/3$ of 1, equals $5/6$ of 1. Or it may mean that $1/2$ of something, plus $1/3$ of that same thing, equals $5/6$ of that same thing, whatever the thing is.

---

[1] Almost all of them said just this.

But wait a minute. Are not all numbers operators? When we say $2 + 3 = 5$, do we not mean that 2 somethings plus 3 somethings equal 5 of those things? In short, when we teach arithmetic, are we not always teaching algebra whether we know it or not? And may not some of our difficulties and confusions arise from the fact that we don't know it, are not aware of it? When we write $2 + 2 = 4$, what we really mean is $2x + 2x = 4x$.

We are used to the idea that we cannot add fractions unless we have common denominators. But this is true of whole numbers as well. Example: 2 horses + 3 horses = 5 horses; but 2 horses + 3 freight trains = what?—5 objects, 5 things, perhaps. But then, we have given horses and freight trains the common denominator, objects.[1]

I have long suspected that there is more to this business of "understanding" arithmetic than meets the eye, and I am just now beginning to get an inkling of how much more. There is nothing particularly simple about "simple" arithmetic. The idea that any nice, sympathetic woman can, without further thought, teach children to "understand" arithmetic is just plain foolish.

March 8, 1959

The doctrine of this school seems to be that if children make pictures to illustrate their work with

---

[1] Three years later, and without having given the children any preparation, I wrote on the blackboard of a first grade class: 2 horses + 3 cows = ? A number of the children gave me the answer, "Five animals."

fractions, they will understand what they are doing and will not make mistakes. The other day I saw an interesting example of this theory in operation. Pat had the problem $\frac{1}{2} + \frac{1}{3} = ?$ She thought about it a while, then drew two rectangles, each divided in thirds. She shaded two sections of one rectangle, and wrote, "This is $\frac{1}{2}$." Then she shaded one section of the other, and wrote, "This is $\frac{1}{3}$." She looked at them a bit; then she wrote "$\frac{1}{2} + \frac{1}{3} = 1$ whole." And she sat back with a pleased and satisfied look on her face.

Hester wrote, "$\frac{1}{2} + \frac{1}{3} = \frac{3}{4}$." Barbara, sitting next to her, instantly said, "No! $\frac{1}{3}$ isn't the same as $\frac{1}{4}$." It took me a second or two to see what she meant. Since $\frac{1}{2} + \frac{1}{4} = \frac{3}{4}$, $\frac{1}{2} + \frac{1}{3}$ cannot equal $\frac{3}{4}$. This child looks at everything she does from several different angles to see whether it fits together and makes sense. But how rare, how very rare she is.

I asked Monica the other day how many thirds were in one whole. She said, "It depends on how big the whole is." If we could look into the minds of our students, in how many would we find that thought? They know it is *wrong* and mustn't be said; but how many think it in silence?

Sometimes Pat is in touch with the real world. I asked her, "Would you rather have $\frac{1}{3}$ or $\frac{1}{4}$ of something to eat?" She said in a flash, "Depends what it is."

Right after vacation, I gave everyone in the afternoon section rods and asked them to figure out what $\frac{1}{2} + \frac{1}{3}$ would be. I don't remember giving them any hints; I'm almost sure I did not. Most of the class, without hints, shuffled the rods around until they found or made a 6 cm. or 12 cm.

length, found half of it and a third of it, added them, and gave me the answer ⅚. I am almost afraid to try it again. Some of them might be able to do this without the rods; most of them, not.

Betty said, "¾ + ⅗ is 1 or more. You need two more fifths to make 1, and ¾ is more than ⅖, so the answer must be bigger than 1." A remarkable kid. And yet, in a conventional school, she might have been considered a "slow" pupil, and might have become one.[1] She *likes* to look at things from several angles, to consider the meaning, or meanings of what she is doing before she does it. But on the whole, this is not the way to get ahead in school.

Later she asked someone, "What's a third of 20—without any halves?"

Still later, they were working on ½ + ¼, and I heard these remarks:

Ralph: It's ¾, and don't ask us how we did it.

Gil: Add 1 and 1 and you get 3?

Betty: I'm not doing it *that* way, I'm doing it *the* way.

Later, working on ⅕ + ³⁄₁₀:

Betty: Answer is ⁵⁄₁₀ or ½.

Gil: But 5 isn't half of 10 and 10 isn't half of 3.

Jane said thoughtfully to herself, "Eight goes into 24 three times. Three goes into 24 how many times?" It took her a long time to figure this out.

Incidentally, in spite of the school crusade against "goes into," all the children say it, without exception.

---

[1] Later, some of her math teachers *did* consider her a slow pupil.

April 24, 1959

If children come to feel that the universe does not make sense, it may be because the language we use to talk about it does not seem to make sense, or at least because there are contradictions between the universe as we experience it and as we talk about it.

One of the main things we try to do in school is to give children a tool—language—with which to learn, think, and talk about the world they live in. Or rather, we try to help them refine the tool they already have. We act as if we thought this tool of language were perfect, and children had only to learn to use it correctly—*i.e.* as we do. In fact, it is in many ways a most imperfect tool. If we were more aware of its imperfections, of the many ways in which it does not fit the universe it attempts to describe, of the paradoxes and contradictions built into it, then we could warn the children, help them see where words and experience did not fit together, and perhaps show them ways of using language that would to some extent rise above its limitations.

Look at adjectives—some are, so to speak, absolute: round, blue, green, square. But many others are relative: long, short, thin, thick, heavy, light, high, low, near, far, easy, hard, loud, soft, hot, cold. None of these have any absolute meaning. Long and short only mean longer and shorter than something else. But we use these words as if they were absolutes. In fact, there must be many times when a child hears a particular thing called long

one day and short the next, or hot one day and cold
the next. We use words as if they were fixed in
meaning, but we keep changing the meanings. The
soup that has become cold is still too hot for the
baby. The short pencil today is the long pencil
tomorrow. The big kitty's name is Midnight; but
don't be rough with him, he's too little. Horses are
big animals; see the little horsie (three times the
size of the child). How big you've grown; you
can't have that, you're too little. Children adjust
to this kind of confusion; but is it an intellectually
healthy and useful adjustment, or just a kind of
production strategy? Would it be useful to talk
to first graders about why we call a certain mountain small and a certain kitten big? Or is this easy
stuff for them?

The conventional teaching of grammar adds to
the confusion. We talk about, and use, nouns and
adjectives as if they were very different, but in
fact they are often very much alike. A green ball,
a green top, a green bicycle, and a green stuffed
animal are alike in that they are green (adjective)
and that they are toys (noun). When we call them
green, we mean they are members of a class that
have in common the color green. When we call
them toys we mean that they are members of a
class that have in common the fact that children
play with them. Why should a child be expected
to feel that there is something very different about
these classes? Why is the green-ness of a ball
different from the ball-ness of a ball? I don't feel
the difference. They are both ways of saying something about the object. We tell children that the
distinction between one part of speech and an-

other is a matter of meaning, when it really has to do with the way we fit them into sentences.

April 30, 1959

Nat said the other day, when asked how he did a certain problem with fractions, "I find it almost always has some diagonal form." He was looking for a rule to fit all cases with no thought of what fractions actually represent. Elaine, given fractions to add, still adds the tops and the bottoms (+ means add, so when you see a +, you add everything in sight).

I watched Nat working on $\frac{1}{3} + \frac{1}{4} = ?$ He started writing equivalent fractions for $\frac{1}{3}-\frac{2}{6}$, $\frac{4}{12}$, $\frac{8}{24}$, etc. Using this doubling process, he wrote a long string of fractions. Then he did the same for $\frac{1}{4}-\frac{2}{8}$, $\frac{4}{16}$, $\frac{8}{32}$. But he couldn't figure out why he couldn't get a common denominator for both fractions. Sam had to show him that $\frac{1}{4}$ could be written as $\frac{6}{24}$.

Rule following! Some of these kids are like a man traveling across open country in a tank. They look out at the world through a tiny peephole, point themselves at a target and start off, but if a bump throws them off course and they lose sight of the target, they're lost. They don't know where they started from, how far they have gone, or where they are.

A first grader was doing a page of problems in a workbook. The answers were given, but some were right, others not, and the child was supposed to mark them accordingly. He marked the first three or four correct, then put an X by the next one. He did it so quickly that the teacher asked how he knew it was wrong. He said, "Oh, they always put a wrong one about here."

June 15, 1959

Kids in school seem to use a fairly consistent strategy. Even the good students use it much of the time; the bad students use it all the time; and everyone uses it when they feel under pressure. One way of describing this strategy is to say that it is answer-centered rather than problem-centered. The difference can best be seen by comparing the way in which the two kinds of people deal with a problem.

The problem-centered person sees a problem as a statement about a situation, from which something has been left out. In other words, there is in this situation a relationship or consequence that has not been stated and that must be found. He attacks the problem by thinking about the situation, by trying to create it whole in his mind. When he sees it whole, he knows which part has been left out, and the answer comes almost by itself. The answer to any problem, school problem, is in the problem, only momentarily hidden from view. Finding it is like finding a missing piece in a jigsaw puzzle. If you look at the empty space in the puzzle, you know the shape of the piece that must fill it.

But most children in school are answer-centered rather than problem-centered. They see a problem as a kind of announcement that, far off in some mysterious Answerland, there is an answer, which they are supposed to go out and find. Some children begin right away to try to pry this answer out of the mind of the teacher. Little children are good at this. They know, especially if they are cute-looking, that if they look baffled or frightened enough, teacher will usually tell them what they need to know. This is called "helping them." Bolder children are ready to sally forth into Answerland in a kind of treasure hunt for the answer. For them, the problem is an answer-getting recipe, a set of hints or clues telling them what to do, like instructions for finding buried pirate treasure— go to the big oak, walk a hundred paces in line with the top of the church steeple, etc. These *producers* think, "Let's see, what did I do last time I had a problem like this?" If they remember their recipes, and don't mix them up, they may be good at the answer-hunting game, and the answers they bring home may often be right ones.

Take the problem, "Ann is three years older than Mary, and their ages add up to 21. How old is each?" The problem-centered person tries to make these girls real in his mind. Are they grown up? No; their ages will add up to too much. They have to be about 10. All but a few of the possible Annes and Marys disappear, and the correct pair looms up larger and larger, until there they are, aged 9 and 12.

The problem-centered person may use a formula. He might see very quickly that Ann's and Mary's ages added up to twice Mary's age, plus three. He might even write down something like $A + M = 21; M + M + 3 = 21; 2 M = 18;$ so $M = 9$ and $A =$

12. But the point is that he would get this formula, this problem-solving process, *out of the problem itself*, not out of his memory.

The answer-centered person, on the other hand, the skilled one, not the coaxer of teachers or the reader of teachers' minds, thinks, "Now let me see, how are we supposed to do this kind of problem? When did I have one like it? Oh yes, I remember, you write down something about their ages, let's see, let x equal Mary's age, then we have to let Ann's age be something, I guess $x + 3$, then what do we do, add them together, maybe, yes, that's right, $x + x + 3 = 21$, then we have to transpose the 3, how do we do that, subtract from both sides . . ." and so on until he gets an answer which he takes to the teacher and says, "Is this right?" But this answer was *elsewhere*, not in the problem, and the answer-getting process had to be dredged up out of blind memory.

Practically everything we do in school tends to make children answer-centered. In the first place, right answers pay off. Schools are a kind of temple of worship for "right answers," and the way to get ahead is to lay plenty of them on the altar. In the second place, the chances are good that teachers themselves are answer-centered, certainly in mathematics, but by no means only there. What they do, they do because this is what they were or are told to do, or what the book says to do, or what they have always done. In the third place, even those teachers who are not themselves answer-centered will probably not see, as for many years I did not, the distinction between problem-centeredness, far less understand its importance. Thus their ways of teaching children, and, above all, the sheer volume of work they give them, will force the children into answer-directed strategies, if only because there isn't time for anything else. I have noticed many times that when the workload of the class is light, kids are willing to do some thinking, to take time to figure things out; when the workload is heavy, the "I-don't-get-it" begins to sound, the thinking stops, they expect us to show them everything. Thus one ironical consequence of the drive for so-called higher standards in schools is that the children are too busy to think.

The other day I was working with a sixteen-year-old boy who was having trouble with first-year physics. I asked him to do one of the problems in his book. Immediately he began to write on his paper, "Given": then, under it, "To Find": and under that, "Use." He began to fill in these spaces with a hash of letters and figures. I said, "Whoa, hold on, you don't even know what the problem is about, at least think about it before you start writing down a mess of stuff." He said, "But our teacher tells us we have to do all our problems this way." So there we are. No doubt this teacher would say that he wants his students to think about problems, and that he prescribed this form so that they would think. But what he has not seen, and probably never will see, is that his means to the end of clearer thinking has become an end in itself, just part of the ritual mumbo-jumbo you have to go through on your answer-hunt.

When kids are in a situation where they are not under pressure to come up with a right answer, far less do it quickly, they can do amazing things. Last fall, about November, I gave the afternoon section some problems. I said, "You have never seen problems like these, you don't know how to do them, and I don't care whether you get them right or not. I just want to see how you go about trying to do them." The problems were basically simple algebra problems, like the one about Ann and Mary, or a certain number of nickels and dimes adding up to 85 cents—the kind of problem that many first-year algebra students find so difficult. These fifth graders tore into them with imagination, resourcefulness, and common sense—in a word, intelligently. They solved them in many ways, including some I hadn't thought of. But it was about that time that the school began to worry about my going too slowly. Soon I was told to speed up the pace, which I am ashamed to say I did, and the children lapsed right back into their old strategies. Probably for keeps.

October 1, 1959

Not long ago Dr. Gattegno taught a demonstration class at Lesley-Ellis School. I don't believe I will ever forget it. It was one of the most extraordinary and moving spectacles I have seen in all my life.

The subjects chosen for this particular demonstration were a group of severely retarded children. There were about five or six fourteen- or fifteen-year-olds. Some of them, except for unusually expressionless faces, looked quite normal; the one who caught my eye was a boy at the end of the table. He was tall, pale, with black hair. I have rarely seen on a human face such anxiety and tension as showed on his. He kept darting looks around the room like a bird, as if enemies might come from any quarter left unguarded for more than a second. His tongue worked continuously in his mouth, bulging out first one cheek and then the other. Under the table, he scratched—or rather clawed—at his leg with one hand. He was a terrifying and pitiful sight to see.

With no formalities or preliminaries, no ice-breaking or jollying up, Gattegno went to work. It will help you see more vividly what was going on if, providing you have rods at hand, you actually do the operations I will describe. First he took two blue (9) rods,[1] and between them put a dark green (6), so that between the two blue rods and above the dark green there was an empty space 3 cm. long. He said to the group, "Make one like this." They did. Then he said, "Now find the rod that will just fill up that space." I don't know how the other children worked on the problem; I was watching the dark-haired boy. His movements were spasmodic, feverish. When he had picked a rod out of the pile in the center of the table, he could hardly stuff it in between his blue rods. After several trials, he and the others found that a light green (3) rod would fill the space.

Then Gattegno, holding his blue rods at the upper end, shook them, so that after a bit the dark green rod fell out. Then he turned the rods over, so that now there was a 6 cm. space where the dark green rod had formerly been. He asked the class to do the same. They did. Then he asked them to find the rod that would fill that space. Did they pick out of the pile the dark green rod that had just come out of that space? Not one did.

[1] See footnote, pp. 106-107.

Instead, more trial and error. Eventually, they all found that the dark green rod was needed.

Then Gattegno shook his rods so that the light green fell out, leaving the original empty 3 cm. space, and turned them again so that the empty space was uppermost. Again he asked the children to fill the space, and again, by trial and error, they found the needed light green rod. As before, it took the dark-haired boy several trials to find the right rod. These trials seemed to be completely haphazard.

Hard as it may be to believe, Gattegno went through this cycle at least four or five times before anyone was able to pick the needed rod without hesitation and without trial and error. As I watched, I thought, "What must it be like to have so little idea of the way the world works, so little feeling for the regularity, the orderliness, the sensibleness of things?" It takes a great effort of the imagination to push oneself back, back, back to the place where we knew as little as these children. It is not just a matter of not knowing this fact or that fact; it is a matter of living in a universe like the one lived in by very young children, a universe which is utterly whimsical and unpredictable, where nothing has anything to do with anything else—with this difference, that these children had come to feel, as most very young children do not, that this universe is an enemy.

Then, as I watched, the dark-haired boy *saw!* Something went "click" inside his head, and for the first time, his hand visibly shaking with excitement, he reached without trial and error for the right rod. He could hardly stuff it into the empty space. It worked! The tongue going round in the mouth, and the hand clawing away at the leg under the table doubled their pace. When the time came to turn the rods over and fill the other empty space, he was almost too excited to pick up the rod he wanted; but he got it in. "It fits! It fits!" he said, and held up the rods for all of us to see. Many of us were moved to tears, by his excitement and joy, and by our realization of the great leap of the mind he had just taken.

After a while, Gattegno did the same problem, this time using a crimson (4) and yellow (5) rod between the blue rods. This time the black-haired boy needed only one cycle to convince himself that these were the rods he needed. This time he was calmer, surer; he knew.

Again using the rods, Gattegno showed them what we mean when we say that one thing is half of another. He used the white (1) and red (2), and the red and the crimson (4) to demonstrate the meaning of "half." Then he asked them to find half of some of the other rods, which the dark-haired boy was able to do. Just before the end of the demonstration Gattegno showed them a brown (8) rod and asked them to find half of half of it, and this too the dark-haired boy was able to do.

I could not but feel then, as I do now, that whatever his I.Q. may be considered to have been, and however he may have reacted to life as he usually experienced it, this boy, during that class, had played the part of a person of high intelligence and had done intellectual work of very high quality. When we think of where he started, and where he finished, of the immense amount of mathematical territory that he covered in forty minutes or less, it is hard not to feel that there is an extraordinary capacity locked up inside that boy.

It is the tragedy of his life that he will probably never again find himself with a man like Gattegno, who knows, as few teachers do, that it is his business to put himself into contact with the intelligence of his students, wherever and whatever that may be, and who has enough intuition and imagination to do it. He has not done much work with retarded children, but he saw in a moment what I might have taken days or weeks to find out, or might never have found out: that to get in touch with the intelligence of these children, to give them solid ground to stand and move on, he had to go way, way back, to the very beginning of learning and understanding. Nor was this all he brought to the session. Equally important was a kind of respect for these children, a conviction that under the right circumstances they could and would do first-class thinking. There was no condescension or pity in his manner, nor even any noticeable sympathy. For the duration of the class he and these children were no less than colleagues, trying to work out a tough problem—and working it out.

February 14, 1960

I gave Edward a handful of rods and asked, "How many whites would you need to make this many?" He arranged the rods in 10 cm. rows, making 15 rows of 10 and a crimson (4) left over. Then he began to count the rows, counting by tens—a sensible procedure—saying, as he touched each row, "10, 20, 30 . . ." and so on up to 100. Then, to my utter astonishment, he said, as he touched the remaining five rows of 10 and the crimson, "200, 300, 400, 500, 600, 604."

I asked him to try again. He assumed that he had made a mistake. This time he counted, as before, up to 100, then, as he touched the remaining rows, said, "101, 102, 103, 104, 105, 109." But he did not look satisfied with this.

The next time Edward began to count the rows of 10, he said, "I'll call each one of these rows 1." However, when he got to the tenth row of 10, he called it 1000, and called each additional row 100, so that his answer was in the 1500's. After fiddling with this a bit, he went back to his original system, and after getting the answer 604 several times, said with assurance that it was right.

I split the group of rods into two sections, ten rows of 10 in one, five rows of 10, and the crimson, in the other. I asked how much was in each group. After counting, he said there was 100 in the large group, and 54 in the small. I slid the two groups together and asked how many there were in all. He went through his usual routine and said again, "604."

I took away the crimson rod, again split the rods into a group of 100 and a group of 50, and asked how many were in each. Again he told me there were 100 in the large group and 50 in the small. When I slid them together, he told me there were 600.

I then put out 100. "How many are there?" "100." I added a white rod, and asked, "How many now?" "101" I added another white rod, and asked, "How many now?" "102" And so up to 109. But then, when I added one more white rod, giving me eleven rows of 10, and asked how many there were, he said, "200."

I said, "OK, let's quit for today."

Now Edward's former teachers gave him many hours of special, individual "help" on arithmetic. But their help consisted in trying to get him to learn the recipes for the problems that he was supposed to know how to do. None of them tried to find out, as for years I never did, just what he did know about numbers, what sort of mental model he had of the world of numbers and how they behaved. As a matter of fact, this boy, if he is feeling good, can carry out correctly quite a number of arithmetic recipes; he is by no means the worst in the class in this respect. But this knowledge is apparent, not real.

The distinction is vital, yet many teachers do not seem to know that it exists. They think, if a child doesn't know how to multiply, you show him how, and give him practice and drill. If he still makes mistakes, you show him how again, and give more practice. If, after you have done this about a dozen times, he still makes mistakes, you assume that he is either unable or unwilling to learn—as one teacher put it, either stupid, lazy, disorganized, or emotionally disturbed. We do not consider that such a child may be unable to learn because he does not grasp the fundamental nature of the symbols he is working with. If numbers themselves are meaningless, how can multiplication be meaningful? Trying to teach such children to multiply, divide, etc., is like trying to build a ten-story building on a foundation of old cardboard boxes. With the best will in the world, it can't be done.

The foundation must be rebuilt first. Children like Edward, and there are many, would not be in the spot he is in if, all along the line, their teachers had been concerned to build slowly and solidly, instead of trying to make it look as if the children knew all the material that was supposed to be covered.

The other day I asked the class to find a number of pairs of numbers, of which the smaller was one-fifth of the larger. Edward wrote 1, 5, and then 5, 25. Then he looked at the 1, 5 for a while. It occurred to him to try the system of adding 1 to each number, giving him the pairs, 2, 6; 3, 7; 4, 8; and so on. And that is what he wrote down. The original problem was forgotten, had turned into something else. Edward's unsteerable mental wagon had been bumped off course and was now rolling in a new direction.

One reason children like this have trouble checking their work is that checking requires you to look at, and keep in mind, two very different things—what you are doing, and what you meant to do, what you ought to be doing. Edward shifts his focus of attention so slowly that when he has figured out what he was *supposed* to be doing, he has forgotten what he *was* doing, and vice versa. I sometimes imagine him dialing a phone number. He has it written before him. He looks at it, and begins to dial. By the time he has dialed two or three digits, he has forgotten the rest of the number. He looks back at the paper, and reminds himself of the number; but by now he has forgotten how much he has already dialed, and must begin again. Maybe Edward doesn't do this with phones, but it is exactly how he does his math. I can often hear him muttering to himself, "Let's see, where was I?"

When I asked for pairs of numbers, one of them half of the other, he wrote: "1 is half of 2; 2 is half of 4; 4 is half of 6; 6 is half of 8." For one-third, he wrote: "3 is one-third of 6; 1 is one-third of 6; 6 is one-third of 12; 12 is one-third of 18." Then, later: "1 is one-fourth of 4; 10 is one-fourth of 40; 40 is one-fourth of 70; 70 is one-fourth of 100; etc." Or "7 is half of 14; 14 is half of 21; 21 is half of 28, etc." The only meaningful relationship he can see between two numbers is the additive one. Perhaps the reason is that he relies so heavily on counting, which is an additive operation.

Edward has acquired the habit of acting unintelligently in math class because for years he has not really known what he was doing. This unintelligent behavior has become fixed, and would be hard to change. But, remembering Gattegno and those retarded children, I think it might be done. Intelligence can be destroyed; perhaps it can also be rebuilt.

March 2, 1960

A child who has really learned something can use it, and does use it. It is connected with reality in his mind, therefore he can make other connections between it and reality when the chance comes. A piece of unreal learning has no hooks on it; it can't be attached to anything, it is of no use to the learner.

Our first graders are using the rods. They know them by name and by length. They are used to calling the orange rod the 10 rod, a bad habit which we can't break them of. They can count up to 100 or higher. They have been told, and many of them can repeat, the usual school rigmarole about tens, units, and so forth. The other day I thought I would see how many of them grasped and could use the fact that a number like 38 could be represented by three orange (10) rods and a brown (8). One at a time, I asked them, if we started at the edge of their desk, how far across a row of 38 whites would reach. One little girl immediately took out three orange rods and a brown, lined them up, and showed me. Her expression said clearly, "What's so hard about that?" Every other child out of seven or eight, including most of the able children in the class, tried to do it by lining up white rods, usually losing count several times in the process.

This suggests that though the children call the dark green rod 6 they do not fully grasp that it is equivalent to 6 whites—even though they could probably tell you so if you asked them. Six is just a name that the dark green happens to have; it has nothing to do with its size in relation to some other rod. They look at the rods as another kind of numeral, symbols made of colored wood rather than marks on paper. Asked $5 + 4 = ?$, they take the rod named 5 and the rod named 4, put them end to end, and find that they match the rod whose name is 9; but they don't grasp the way in which this kind of operation is the same as the operation of combining a group of 5 and another group of 4 separate objects.

Some second graders, given problems like $59 + 42 + 35$, got their carrying mixed up and got answers in the 1200's, or higher. They seemed perfectly satisfied. One reason they did not know that 1200 was too big is that they do not know how big 1200 is. We can't expect children to work sensibly with numbers, checking their work against some notion of reality, when we ask them to do calculations involving magnitudes they do not understand. Perhaps we should ask more questions like: How long a row would 38 (or 50, 75, 100, 200, 500, 1000) white rods make, put side by side? How many white rods would be needed to cover given rectangles, a piece of paper, the top of a desk, the floor of a room? How many whites would be needed to fill boxes of various sizes?

The children are willing to accept all kinds of mathematical shorthand if I tell them that I am too lazy to write out things the long way. In the first place, this is true. In the second place, it gives them a chance to make fun of my laziness, and to feel (which is also true) that in accepting my shorthand they are doing me a kind of favor. They do not like to be told that a certain symbol "means" something. This seems arbitrary and mysterious. But if you express a relationship or an operation in terms with which they are familiar, they will soon be perfectly willing to let you use some kind of shorthand to express it. Thus we can go from "Two whites are as long as one red" to "2 whites = 1 red" to "$2 \times w = r$."

After all, men invented mathematical symbols to save the trouble of writing things out the long way, so what I am doing in class is both logically and historically correct. No symbol "means" anything until we decide and agree to let it mean something; so why not let children feel that they are in on this decision?

We make a serious mistake in asking children to perform symbolically operations which they could not perform concretely. A child should be able to find out which has the most whites, a group of 37 or a group of 28, and how many more it has, before he is asked to do a problem like 37 — 28 = ?, and he should be able to do this latter kind of problem easily before he is given a rule for doing it. So with all the operations of arithmetic. Numerical arithmetic should look to children like a simpler and faster way of doing things that they know how to do already, not a set of mysterious recipes for getting right answers to meaningless questions.

April 16, 1960

There are sixteen kids in my math class. Four are poor students; one is fair; all the rest are exceptionally bright and able, with a good feel for math. They have all had place value explained to them many times.

The other day I asked, "Suppose I go to the bank with a check for $1437.50, cash it, and ask them to give me as much of the money as possible in ten dollar bills. How many tens will I get?" I wrote the number on the board. After some scrambling around for pencils and scratch paper, answers began to appear. None were correct; most were wildly off. A few kids got the answer on the second or third try; most never got it.

I erased the original number from the board, and wrote $75.00. "How many tens will you get?" Everyone knew. I then wrote $175.00. "Now how many?" This was much harder; a few got it, most did not. After a while, pointing to the digit 7 in 175, I asked, "What does this 7 tell me?" They said it meant that I had 70 dollars, or 7 tens. I wrote it on the board. Then I said, "Now how about this 1?" They all said that it meant that we had a hundred dollars. Nobody said that it meant just as well that we had ten more tens. I said, "How many tens could we get for that hundred?" They all said 10. I pointed out that these 10 tens, plus the 7 they had already told us about, would give us 17 tens. I then wrote our first number—$1437.50—on the board. We considered how many tens were represented by each digit. The 3 told us we had 3 tens; the 4, that we had 40 more; the 1, that we had 100 more, for a total of 143 tens. I drew a circle around the digits 143 in the numeral 1437. By this time everyone was saying, "Oh, yeah, I get it; I see; it's easy; it's cinchy." But I was skeptical, believing no longer in the magic power of "good explanations."

Two days later I wrote on the board $14357.50, and asked how many hundred dollar bills I could get if I cashed a check for that much. Some answers were 43, 17, 107, 142, 604, 34, 13100, and 22. Only one student got the answer the first time. Four more eventually got it, before I worked it on the board. The other eleven were completely stumped. Again, I put the numeral 14357 on the board, and went through digit by digit, showing how many hundreds were represented by each digit, and therefore, how many hundreds were in the entire number. But I doubt that they understand place value any better than they did before.

This lack of understanding makes long division hard, or impossible, for many children. Take the problem, 260 divided by 5. We cannot divide 2 hundreds evenly among five people, so we must change them into something that we can divide. We exchange our 2 hundreds for 20 tens. We now have 26 tens in all. We divide 25 of these among our five people, giving them five 10's each. We have one 10 left, which we exchange for ten 1's, which we divide among our five people, so that they have five 10's and two 1's apiece. Our way of doing long division depends on this idea of making change, and a child who does not know that this is what he is doing, or why he is doing it, will see long division, as most children do, as a meaningless recipe which will give him endless trouble.

June 20, 1960

How can we tell whether children understand something or not? When I was a student, I generally knew when I understood and when I didn't. This had nothing to do with marks; in the last math course I took in college I got a respectable grade, but by the end of the year I realized I didn't have the faintest idea of what the course was about. In Colorado, I assumed for a long time that my students knew when they did, or did not, understand something. I was always urging them to tell me when they did not understand, so that with one of my clever "explanations" I could clear up everything. But they never would tell me. I came to know by painful experience that not a child in a hundred knows whether or not he understands something, much less, if he does not, why he does not. The child who knows, we don't have to worry about; he will be an A student. How do we find out when, and what, the others don't understand?

What first comes to mind is some external test. But what kind? By now I have many times seen children crank out right answers to problems without the faintest idea of what they were doing. They are blind recipe-followers. Some can even parrot back my explanations, but again without knowing what they mean. On the other hand, there are many children who are so paralyzed by their fear of tests that they can't show what they do know, while others who understand clearly what they are doing get confused and scared when they try to put it into words.

Part of the answer to the problem may be to give children the kind of tests I used this year, in which there was a mixture of problems. These tend to throw the automatic answer-finding machinery out of gear and to make them do some thinking about what they are doing. It may help, too, to give problems in a form new to them. But what do we do when the result of such tests is to show that hardly any of our pupils understand anything of what we have been trying to teach them during the year?

It may help to have in our minds a picture of what we mean by understanding. I feel I understand something if and when I can do some, at least, of the following: (1) state it in my own words; (2) give examples of it; (3) recognize it in various guises and circumstances; (4) see connections between it and other facts or ideas; (5) make use of it in various ways; (6) foresee some of its consequences; (7) state its opposite or converse. This list is only a beginning; but it may help us in the future to find out what our students really know as opposed to what they can give the appearance of knowing, their *real learning* as opposed to their *apparent learning*.

There are many, of course, who say that this distinction does not exist. It's their handy way of solving the knotty problem of understanding; just say there is no such thing. Apparently this view is currently in fashion among psychologists. According to many of them, if you can say that $7 \times 8 = 56$, you know all there is to know about that particular fact, and you know as much about it as anyone else who can say it. The mathematician, the third grader, and, presumably, a well-trained parrot, would all have an equal and identical understanding of this fact. The only difference between the mathematician and the child is that the mathematician carries around in his head many more such facts. So to make children into mathematicians all we have to do is train them, condition them, until they can say many such facts. Teach them to say everything that Einstein knew, and hey, presto! another Einstein!

It's amazing what nonsense people will believe.

Of course, this notion fits neatly into behaviorism, which is also still very much in fashion, despite all it cannot explain. It is also comforting to teachers, who have felt all along that their job is to drop, or push, one at a time, little bits of information into those largely empty minds that are moving slowly before them down the academic assembly line. And finally, it has set into motion the apparently endless gravy train of programed instruction and machine teaching, onto which everyone and his brother seem to be happily clambering.

But pieces of information like $7 \times 8 = 56$ are not isolated facts. They are parts of the landscape, the territory of numbers, and that person knows them best who sees most clearly how they fit into the landscape and all the other parts of it. The mathematician knows, among many other things, that $7 \times 8 = 56$ is an illustration of the fact that products of even integers are even; that 7×8 is the same as 14×4 or 28×2 or 56×1; that only these pairs of positive integers will give 56 as a product; that 7×8 is $(8 \times 8) - 8$, or $(7 \times 7) + 7$, or $(15 \times 4) - 4$; and so on. He also knows that $7 \times 8 = 56$ is a way of expressing in symbols a relationship that may take many forms in the world of real objects; thus he knows that a rectangle 8 units long and 7 units wide will have an area of 56 square units. But the child who has learned to say like a parrot, "Seven times eight is fifty-six" knows nothing of its relation either to the real world or to the world of numbers. He has nothing but blind memory to help him. When memory fails, he is perfectly capable of saying that $7 \times 8 = 23$, or that 7×8 is smaller than 7×5, or larger than 7×10. Even when he knows 7×8, he may not know 8×7, he may say it is something quite different. And when he remembers 7×8, he cannot use it. Given a rectangle of 7 cm. $\times$ 8 cm., and asked how many 1 sq. cm. pieces he would need to cover it, he will over and over again cover the rectangle with square pieces and laboriously count them up, never seeing any connection between his answer and the multiplication tables he has memorized.

Knowledge, learning, understanding, are not linear. They are not little bits of facts lined up in rows or piled up one on top of another. A field of knowledge, whether it be math, English, history, science, music, or whatever, is a territory, and knowing it is not just a matter of knowing all the items in the territory, but of knowing how they relate to, compare with, and fit in with each other. It is the difference between being able to say that a room in your house has so many tables, so many chairs, so many lamps, and being able to close your eyes and see that this chair goes here and that table there. It is the difference between knowing the names of all the streets in a city and being able to get from any place, by any desired route, to any other place.

Why do we talk and write about the world and our knowledge of it as if they were linear? Because that is the nature of talk. Words come out in single file, one at a time; there's no other way to talk or write. So, in order to talk about it, we cut the real, undivided world into little pieces, and make these into strings of talk, like beads on a necklace. But we must not be fooled; these strings of talk are not what the world is like. Our learning is not real, not complete, not accurate, above all not useful, unless we take these word strings and somehow convert them in our minds into a likeness of the world, a working mental model of the universe as we know it. Only when we have made such a model, and when there is at least a rough correspondence between that model and reality, can it be said of us that we have learned something.

What happens in school is that children take in these word strings and store them, undigested, in their minds, so that they can spit them back out on demand. But these words do not change anything, fit with anything, relate to anything. They are as empty of meaning as parrot-speech is to a parrot. How can we make school a place where real learning goes on, and not just word swallowing?

September 11, 1960

During a visit, two friends asked me to do some math with their ten-year-old daughter, who was having some trouble. I said OK; the child and I have been friends for many years, and I thought I might be able to find out something about her way of thinking about arithmetic problems. I began with mental arithmetic. I planned to ask her 2×76, and when she had given the answer, 2×77. I wanted to see whether she would just add 2 to her first answer, or whether she would treat the second problem as if it was brand new. But I was set back when she told me that 2×76 was 432.

After some mental calculating, I saw that in doing this problem in her head she had multiplied the 2 by the 6, and then the 7 by the 6; in short, that she had multiplied 6×72—correctly, by the way. I asked her to do it again, and again she said 432, showing how strong is our tendency to repeat our own errors, to keep going in the tracks we have already made.

I then said, "What is 2×100?" She said, "200." I asked for 2×90. 180. 2×80? (Pause) 160. 2×76? 432. 2×70? 140. 2×80? 160. 2×76? 432. 2×100? 200. 2×200? 400. 2×76? 432 . . . Here she stopped, looked at me searchingly, and then said, "Now *wait* a minute." She ran to get pencil and paper, saying, "This doesn't make sense, I'm going to figure this out." On the paper, she worked out that 2×76 was 152.

Something very important happened when she said, "Now wait a minute." She was seeing, perhaps for the first time, that we can ask of an answer to a problem, not just "Is it *right*?" or "Is it *wrong*?" but "Is it *sensible*?" and that we can often see, without yet knowing the right answer, that the answer we have doesn't make any sense, is inconsistent with other things we know to be true.

After a little more work she went to bed, pleased with what she had done. Later, I told her parents about her work, to show the kind of difficulties children get into when they don't know, in general, how numbers behave, and know only unrelated facts and recipes. Her father said he understood more clearly what we were trying to do with Cuisenaire rods; but her mother said, defiantly and angrily, that she couldn't understand all these new ideas, and was going to continue working with her daughter as she had been, by giving her a page of problems to do each day, with the threat that for each problem done wrong she would be given several more problems to do.

This reaction astonishes and rather appalls me. Why should this mother be so eager to have arithmetic applied to her child as a kind of punishment? She reminds me of the many parents I have known who at one time or another have urged me to crack down on their children. Do such people see school as a kind of institutionalized punishment, something unpleasant that we can do to children whether or not they have done anything bad to deserve it? What is it that such people resent so about children?

October 16, 1960

I asked the new fifth-grade class, "How many white rods would you need to make a row all the way across your desk?" Of the class of 15, about half began to use orange (10) rods to measure with. The rest, with one exception, began to line up white rods. When they ran out of whites, they used red (2) rods, but putting them side by side, so that they were, so to speak, acting like whites. When they ran out of reds, they used light greens (3), and so on until they had a row all the way across the desk, which they then counted up.

These children have been using the rods for three weeks or more. They are all accustomed to them, and know the lengths of every rod well enough so that they call them by their lengths. They are used to calling the orange rod *the* 10 *rod.* They know it is as long as 10 whites, but they do not transfer this knowledge to a situation in which it would make their work much easier.

I then asked them, "How many whites would you need to cover up one sheet of pad paper (about 9″ × 6″)?" About ten children began covering the entire sheet of paper with rods. A few of these stopped after a while, realizing that every row was the same length. Some of the rest went on to cover the entire paper, before finding the length of a row and multiplying by the number of rows. Others, after covering the entire paper, added up, rod by rod, the lengths of all the rods they had used to cover it. Two children began to cover their papers with rods, but they stood the rods on end, so that every rod, whatever its length and color, covered only 1 sq. cm. Naturally, they ran out of rods long before the paper was covered; then they didn't know what to do.

Dorothy covered her paper with rods, then told me that 44 whites would be enough to cover it. This was a blind guess. I asked, "How many whites would you need to cover an orange rod?" She said, "Around 8." I said, "Try it and find out." She did, and found that 10 whites would be needed. I then asked how many whites she would need to cover four orange rods. She just stared at me in silence.

October 30, 1960

We did some work the other day on multiplication tables. The results were, to say the least, astonishing. The paper was marked in a grid of 10 × 10 squares, that is, 100 squares arranged in 10 rows, 10 squares in each row. Across the top row, and to the left of the left hand column, were written the numbers from 1 to 10, but in irregular order. Thus every one of the hundred squares in the grid was in a numbered column and a numbered row. If a square was in the row numbered 2 and the column numbered **3**, the child was to put in the square the product of 2×3, or 6. The square in the row numbered **5** and the column numbered **7** would therefore be filled with the number 35. And so on.

From Marjorie's paper, I got: $4 \times 6 = 22$, $4 \times 4 = 20$, $4 \times 7 = 32$. Then, $10 \times 10 = 20$, and right beside it, $10 \times 2 = 22$. Then, side by side in the row numbered **8**, $8 \times 8 = 48$, $8 \times 6 = 59$, $8 \times 4 = 40$, $8 \times 7 = 49$, $8 \times 9 = 42$. In the **7** row, $7 \times 5 = 35$, $7 \times 8 = 24$, $7 \times 7 = 47$, $7 \times 9 = 45$.

I'm not making this up, I swear it!

In the **9** row we have $9 \times 9 = 69$, $9 \times 10 = 40$. In the **4** row, $4 \times 8 = 62$, $4 \times 9 = 40$.

Is it enough to say of this child that she does not know her tables?

November 12, 1960

A few days ago, when I was working with Marjorie, she stopped what she was doing and said, "Can I ask you something?" I said, "Sure, go ahead." She said that when she was adding on her fingers (embarrassed smile) and was counting 10, 11, 12, 13, and so on, sometimes she held up her thumb when she said 10, index finger for 11, middle finger for 12, and then other times she said 11 when she held up her thumb, 12 for index finger, and so on. But one of these methods always gave her the wrong answer, and she could never be sure which. Would I tell her? I said, "Can you give me an example of the kind of problem that might make you do this?" But she could not. This kind of child seldom can.

What she needs is a broom to sweep out her

mind. She has so much junk in there, and her filing systems are in such a mess, that she never can find anything, and the file drawers and old trunks must be emptied out before they can be put into any kind of order. If she could only forget, completely, about nine-tenths of the facts and rules she has all mixed up in her head, she might begin to learn something.

The other day I asked the class to find as many verbs as they could that ended in *p*. Marjorie's face grew panicky as I repeated the instructions. Finally she said, in a near-hysterical voice, "I don't get it." I said, "What don't you get?"—a useless question, but one I can't break myself of asking. She said, as I knew she would, "I just don't get it." I repeated the instructions and asked her to repeat them after me; she did. I then asked if she knew what a verb was. She said she didn't. (She has been given the definition many times.) I gave her some examples of verbs, and she breathed a sigh of relief and went to work. I felt like asking her, "Why didn't you tell me you didn't know what a verb was?" But after some thought, I realized that until I asked her, she did not know herself that she did not know what a verb was. All she knew was that she had been told to start doing something and didn't know what to do. She was wholly incapable of analyzing the instructions, finding out what part of them made sense and what did not, where her knowledge ended and her ignorance began.

Children like Marjorie get in the habit of waiting for teachers to show them how to do everything, so that they may continue by a process of blind imitation; they never learn how to get information out of verbal instructions. In fact, they do not seem to believe that verbal instructions contain information. They do not expect to be able to figure out from mere words what it is that one wants them to do. Nor can they distinguish between the goal and the route needed to get there, the job to be done, and the method needed to do it. If someone gives them a problem, they either know or don't know "how to do it." If they don't, the problem itself is meaningless to them.

And this is the great danger of asking children to manipulate symbols whose concrete meaning they do not understand. After a while they come to feel, like Marjorie, that all symbols are meaningless. Our teaching is too full of words, and they come too soon.

January 26, 1961

I have described (pp. 122 ff.) the problem that Dr. Gattegno gave to his demonstration class of retarded children. The other day I gave this problem to Dorothy, certainly the slowest child I have ever taught. Until now, every child who has tried the problem has done it in one or two tries; she took five or six before she said, "I see what you're doing." When she was able to find the correct rod to fill the empty space, without trial and error or even hesitation, I said, "You're getting too hard to trick," and switched to another game.

Some teachers would wonder what is the point of this kind of game. First, and most important, it gives this child a problem that she can solve, on her own, without help from outside and without recourse to formulas, devices, or recipes dimly remembered and never understood; secondly, it enables her to grasp a fundamental fact about the way in which physical objects behave, a fact which, up until now, she has never grasped, *i.e.*, the behavior of inanimate objects is consistent, reliable, rather than whimsical and unpredictable.

It is easy to feel sometimes that such children have duller senses. It's as if they do not see what we see. Once I asked Dorothy to tell me what rod was the same length as six (or four, or some other number) white rods. Quite often she would take a rod that was two or three centimeters too long or too short, and not be sure that it would not fit until she had carefully put it beside the white rods. Did her senses send her no message until that moment? Or is it that she was afraid to trust such messages as her senses did send?

With enough time, it might be possible to go back to the beginning and rebuild this child's intelligence. Just as mathematics, improperly used, has helped to destroy it, so, properly used, it could help to rebuild it. But this could not be done unless the outside world left her alone while she was learning to make sense of things, and did not try to make her appear to know what she did not know, and did not try to make her feel foolish or ashamed for knowing so little. Clearly this is too much to ask.

January 30, 1961

I asked Andy to make five piles of white rods, with eight in each pile; any small object would have done as well. Then I gave him eight paper cups, and asked him to divide the white rods evenly among the cups. A child who understood multiplication would have known right away that 5 rods were needed for each cup. A somewhat less able child might have said, "5 × 8 = 40; I have 40 rods; if I divide them up among 8 cups I will have 5 rods in each cup." Andy did neither. He started by trying to put 8 rods in each cup, ran out of rods, and said, "That won't work." Then he put 4 rods in each cup, which gave him 8 rods left over. I thought he would distribute these among the 8 cups; to my amazement he emptied all the cups and started all over. Then he tried to put 6 rods in each cup; not enough rods. Then he tried 5 rods per cup, which worked.

One of the beauties of this kind of work is that Andy had no idea, as he struggled toward the solution, that he was making mistakes. In his clumsy way he was doing a piece of research, and without having to be told that it was so, he saw that every unsuccessful attempt brought him closer to the answer he sought. What was, for a fifth grader, a very poor piece of mathematical work, gave him no feeling of failure or shame, but instead a lively satisfaction, something he rarely gets in school.

Ted did some division problems. Given 86 to divide by 2, he had no trouble: 2 into 8 gives 4, 2 into 6 gives 3, so the answer is 43. But when given 96 to divide by 2, he did exactly the same thing: 2 into 9 gives 4, with 1 left over; 2 into 6 gives 3. Again he wrote 43 for the answer. What to do with that leftover 1 he had not the faintest idea. I asked him to divide 55 by 5. His answer was 11.

Then 65. Same answer. Then 75. Same answer. Then 85 and 95. Same answer. He was somewhat uneasy about this, because he said defensively, as if justifying himself, "9 divided by 5 is 1, 5 divided by 5 is 1." But he could not get himself out of the jam.

We did some division by distributing rods among paper cups: I gave him 5 orange (10) and 2 white (1) rods, and asked him to divide them evenly among 4 paper cups. Right away he put 1 orange rod in each cup; then he asked me to give him 10 whites in place of the orange rod he had left over. He then distributed his 12 whites among the four cups, and thus got the correct answer—13.

He did a number of problems like this. Each time he had one or more orange rods left over after he had divided them up among the cups, and each time he asked me to change these left-over rods into whites. Now and then, before giving him his change, I would ask him if he could tell how many of these whites each of his paper cups would get. Quite often he could tell me. Thus, dividing 32 by 2, he put an orange rod in each cup, and then told me, after I had asked him, that the remaining 12 white rods could be divided up 6 to a cup, so that each cup would get a total of 16. But when the divisor was larger than 2 he was uneasy when asked this question, and he never asked it of himself. Each time he wanted all his change in whites, which he painstakingly divided up to get his answer.

This is as it should be. When children are doing concrete operations like this, doing things that they feel are sensible, getting answers by themselves, answers that they can be sure are right, there is much to be said for letting them use a cumbersome method until they feel thoroughly secure in it, before suggesting the possibility that there may be an easier way. It is often said that children find security in drill, in repetitive work. In this kind of situation, where the child is in command, master of his materials and sure of what he is doing, the statement is probably correct. But not one percent of school drill is work of this nature. It is mumbo-jumbo, and the notion that if a child repeats a meaningless statement or process enough times it will become meaningful is as absurd as the notion that if a parrot imitates human speech long enough it will know what it is talking about. This very intelligent boy has been drilled many times in the multiplication tables and the approved method of division, and he is worse off now than the first day he heard them. They make no more sense to him than they ever did, and they scare him a lot more. But if he does these operations enough times with rods, or other materials, so that he can begin to do them in his head without rods, if he can get to the point where he does not have to distribute every last white rod before figuring his answer, we may be able to translate some of these operations into symbols that make some sense to him.

February 3, 1961

Poor Marjorie has tried her best to remember everything anyone has ever told her in school, without being able to make any sense out of any of it, perhaps without even feeling that there was any sense to be made. For her pains, she has a headful of scrambled facts and recipes, few if any of them available on demand, and no idea in the world which of them may be applicable to any given situation.

The other day she asked if she could work with me and the rods. I said, "Sure." First we did the color-rectangle problem: I put some rods together, side by side, to make a rectangle; then I asked her to make a rectangle of the same size, all one color, but using a different color than mine. She saw quickly that it could be done with whites, and soon could do it with other colors as well.

While working she said something that she was to say again many times during the sessions that we worked together—and the written word fails dismally to convey the joy and excitement in her voice—"Oh, this is neat! I love it when you get the trick!"

A day or so later I challenged her to make a rectangle of rods, all one color, such that I could not cover it with a different color (excluding white). After much trial and error she found that she could defeat me with squares of 3, 5, or 7 cm. From this she concluded that one of 9 cm. would do as well, and was surprised when I was able to cover it with light green (3) rods. She did not see that prime numbers were what was needed; but then, though we have been working with prime numbers for weeks, she hasn't a notion of what a prime number is.

Again and again she said how neat it was to get the trick. This is the phrase which she (and not she alone) uses to describe the feeling of having worked something out for yourself and having understood what you did. For all but a few kids in the class, it is an experience so unique that they think of it as having nothing to do with school.

Later we played the division game with paper cups. Like the other children, Marjorie distributed among the cups as many orange and white rods as she could distribute evenly, and then made change with what was left. She liked this game very much, and today had some races with Anna, who is, on the whole, a quicker math student.

These kids would undoubtedly say, if asked, that they were doing division; but they do not think of it that way to themselves, and they do not apply what few division facts they do know. Every time they go through the complicated rigmarole of making change. This suggests that even if we get smart enough to let children do arithmetic operations in the concrete before doing them with symbols—and to get schools and teachers to this point will not be easy—we must still beware of trying to force children into too quick generalizations about what they have been doing. Instead we must find situations in which they will want to find better methods of performing these concrete operations—like the division races between Marjorie and Anna—so that, in the search for better methods, they will make generalizations of their own.

For example, imagine a child who does not know that 42 divided by 3 is 14, and has no recipe for getting the answer. We give him 4 orange and 2 white rods, to divide evenly among 3 cups. He puts an orange rod in each cup, exchanges his remaining orange rod for 10 whites, distributes the 12 whites among the 3 cups, and finds that

each cup has 14. He will do this many times before he sees that, when he has that leftover orange
and 2 whites to divide among three cups, he can
do the rest of the problem in his head without
having to go to the trouble of making change.

The other day I thought I could force this
process. When a child asked me to change an
orange rod into whites, I asked him instead if he
could tell me, without actually making the change
and using the rods, how many whites each cup
would get. If the division factor was one he knew,
he could usually tell me; but it never occurred to
him to do it when I did not ask the question. Left
alone, he went back to his old system, in which
he felt that he knew what he was doing.

We cannot overestimate the importance of this.
The idea of doing the dividing mentally rather
than with white rods did not stick in the minds of
these children because it was my idea, not theirs;
there was no place for it in their minds; it did
not meet any felt intellectual need. We must not
fool ourselves, as for years I fooled myself, into
thinking that guiding children to answers by carefully chosen leading questions is in any important
respect different from just telling them the answers in the first place. Children who have been
led up to answers by teachers' questions are later
helpless unless they can remember the questions,
or ask themselves similar questions, and this is
exactly what they cannot do. The only answer
that really sticks in a child's mind is the answer to
a question that he asked or might ask of himself.

Yesterday we played a different game. I gave
Marjorie 2 white rods, and asked how many dif-

ferently shaped rectangles she could make by putting them together. She saw that there was only one. I added a rod, making 3 rods, and asked her again. Again, only one way to make it. With 4 rods, there were two possible rectangles, a 1 x 4 and a 2 x 2. And so we worked our way up to 20, finding the factors of each number along the way, and noting which numbers were prime. At no time on the way up to 20 did it occur to Marjorie, or the generally more able Anna, that they could solve the problem by making use of what little they knew about factors. Given 10 rods, they did not think, "We can make a rectangle 5 rods long and 2 wide"; they had to work by trial and error each time. But they did get progressively quicker at seeing which combinations were possible and which were not.

I did not see until later that this increased quickness and skill was the beginning, the seed of a generalized understanding. An example comes to mind, that was repeated many times. When the children had 12 rods, they made a 6 x 2 rectangle. Then both of them divided that rectangle in half and put the halves together to make a 4 x 3 rectangle. As they worked, their attack on the problem became more economical and organized. They were a long way from putting their insights and understandings into words, but they were getting there. The essential is that this sort of process not be rushed.

This work has changed most of my ideas about the way to use Cuisenaire rods, and other materials. It seemed to me at first that we could use them as devices for packing in recipes much faster than before, and many teachers seem to be using them this way. But this is a great mistake. What we ought to do is use these materials to enable children to make for themselves, out of their own experience and discoveries, a solid and growing understanding of the ways in which numbers and the operations of arithmetic work. Our aim must be to build soundly, and if this means that we must build more slowly, so be it. Some things we will be able to do much earlier than we used to—fractions, for example. Others, like long division, may have to be put off until later. The work of the children themselves will tell us.

March 11, 1961

Dorothy was working with me the other day. I have been trying to get to the bottom of her misunderstanding of numbers, so that I might find some solid ground to start building on. I think we may have touched the bottom, but it was a long way down.

On the table I made 2 rows of white rods, 5 in each row. As I made them, I said, "Here are 2 rows, same number of rods in each row." She agreed. I asked how many rods I had used to make these 2 rows. She said 10. I wrote 10 on a piece of paper beside us and put a check beside it. Then I made 2 rows of 7. She agreed that the rows were equal, and told me, when I asked, that I had used 14 rods to make them. She had to count them, of course. I wrote 14 and put a check beside it.

Then I said, "Now you make some." She pushed my rows back into the pile, and then brought out some rods, with which she made 2 rows of 6. I

asked how many she had used, and she counted up
to 12. I wrote this down and put a check beside it.
Then I asked her to see if she could make 2 rows
with the same number in each row and no rods left
over, using 11 rods. She pushed her 10 rods back
into the pile, then counted out 11 rods from the
pile and tried to make them into 2 equal rows.
After a while she said, "It won't work." I agreed
that it wouldn't, wrote down 11, and put a big X
beside it.

Then I said, "Some numbers work, like 10 and
14, and others don't, like 11. I'd like you to start
with 6, and tell me which numbers work and
which ones don't." After what we had been doing,
these instructions were clear. She counted out 6
rods, which she made into 2 rows of 3. I wrote
down 6 and checked it. Then I got my first surprise. Instead of bringing out one more rod to give
herself 7, she pushed all of them back into the
pile, then counted out 7 rods, and tried to make 2
equal rows out of them. After a while she said, "It
won't work." I wrote 7, with an X beside it. Then
she pushed all the rods back into the pile, counted
out 8, made 2 rows of 4, and said "8 works." Then
she pushed them all back, counted out 9, could
not make 2 rows, and told me so. And she followed
exactly this procedure all the way up to about 14.

Then she made a big step. Having done 14, she
did not push the rods back into the pile, but
brought out another rod to make 15, and merely
added that rod to one of the rows, before telling
me that 15 would not work. Again she left her
rows, this time adding another rod to the short row,
before telling me that 16 would work. This more
efficient process she continued up into the early

20's—about 24, I think. Then, having found that 24 would work, she said, but without using the rods, "25 won't work." I wrote it, and she continued thus, with increasing speed and confidence, until we got to about 36. At this point she stopped naming the odd numbers altogether, saying only, "36 works, 38 works, 40 works . . ." and so up into the 50's, where we stopped.

We rested a bit, fooled around with the rods, did a little building with them, and then went on to the next problem. This time I made 3 equal rows, and asked her to find what numbers, beginning with 6, would work for this problem. To my surprise, she could not arrange 6 rods in 3 equal rows, arranging them instead in a 3-2-1 pattern. I helped her out, and she began to work. From the start she moved one step ahead of where she had been on the 2-row problem. When I had made 6 rods into 3 rows of 2, and had written that 6 worked, she added a rod to one of the rows, told me that 7 would not work, added a rod to another row, told me that 8 would not work, added a rod to another row, and told me that 9 would work. In this way we worked our way up to about 15 or 18. Here she stopped using the rods, and said, "19 doesn't work, 20 doesn't work, 21 works . . ." and so on. When she got up to about 27, she just gave me the numbers that worked—30, 33, 36, 39.

In the 4-row problem we began with 8 rods. She used the rods to tell me that 9, 10, and 11 would not work, and that 12 would. Without the rods, she told me that 13, 14, and 15 would not work, and that 16 would; from there she began counting by fours—20, 24, 28, 32, etc. In the 5-row problem we began with 10 rods, and after using the rods to get to 15 she went on from there counting by fives.

People to whom I have described this child's work have found it all but impossible to believe. They could not imagine that even the most wildly unsuccessful student could have so little mathematical insight, or would use such laborious and inefficient methods to solve so simple a problem. The fact remains that this is what the child did. There is no use in we teachers telling ourselves that such children *ought* to know more, *ought* to understand better, *ought* to be able to work more efficiently; the facts are what count. The reason this poor child has learned hardly anything in six years of school is that no one ever began where she *was;* just as the reason she was able to make such extraordinary gains in efficiency and understanding during this session is that, beginning where she was, she was learning genuinely and on her own.

March 20, 1961

A number of the children have worked on a problem that could be stated thus, "Find what numbers of squares can be arranged in a rectangle that is more than one square in width?" Clearly, every number except the prime numbers will work for this problem. The other day I turned it into a new and more subtle problem by saying that there had to be a hole, the size of one of the squares, in the exact middle of the rectangle. An able student, like Terry, attacks the problem systematically. He

began by trying to make the smallest possible rectangle with a hole in the center, in short, by
having just one thickness of squares all around
the hole. To do this took 8 squares. Then he considered how this rectangle could grow into a larger
one, while keeping the hole in the middle. He soon
saw that any such rectangle must have sides with
odd lengths—3×5, 7×3, etc. In another moment
he could say, in general, and without any further
construction, which numbers would work and
which would not.

A slow student, like Andy, will attack the problem in an entirely different way. He took 16 rods,
made a 4×4 square, and then spent a long time
trying to remove one rod so that the hole would be
in the middle, but no matter how he shuffled the
rods around, the hole was always in the wrong
place. It was fun to watch him struggle with this;
his failure to get that hole to go where he wanted
exasperated him, but—what is unusual for him—
it did not frighten him. He was working boldly and
determinedly. Eventually, he saw that he would
have to have a rectangle of odd dimensions before
the problem would work. Even then, he did not
see that any such rectangle would do. Compared
with the way Terry tackled the problem, his
method could be called clumsy and inefficient; but
the vital point is that it was his method, exactly
suited to his own store of mathematical learning
and insight; and because it was his own, he was
learning from it.

With thought, practice, and luck we should be
able to devise problems that children can do in
ways which, being their own, will be of use to

them. Such problems could make up a kind of self-adjusting learning-machine, in which the child himself makes the program harder as he becomes more skillful. But this approach to mathematical learning, and other kinds as well, will require teachers to stop thinking of *the* way or *the best* way to solve problems. We must recognize that children who are dealing with a problem in a very primitive, experimental, and inefficient level, are making discoveries that are just as good, just as exciting, just as worthy of interest and encouragement, as the more sophisticated discoveries made by more advanced students. When Dorothy discovers, after long painful effort, that every other number can be divided into 2 equal rows, that every third number can be divided into 3 equal rows, she has made just as great an intellectual leap as those children who, without being told, discovered for themselves some of the laws of exponents.

In other words, the invention of the wheel was as big a step forward as the invention of the airplane—bigger, in fact. We teachers will have to learn to recognize when our students are, mathematically speaking, inventing wheels and when they are inventing airplanes; and we will have to learn to be as genuinely excited and pleased by wheel-inventors as by airplane-inventors. Above all, we will have to avoid the difficult temptation of showing slow students the wheel so that they may more quickly get to work on the airplanes. In mathematics certainly, and very probably in all subjects, knowledge which is not genuinely discovered by children will very likely prove useless and will be soon forgotten.

May 6, 1961

A very skillful public relations job has been done for the so-called new math. Everyone talks about it, and any school or teacher who isn't doing it seems hopelessly old-fashioned. Some of this new math is really very good. Here and there, truly revolutionary and constructive changes in math teaching are being made; children are finding out things for themselves instead of being told answers or hinted toward them with leading questions. But these places are few. Most of the New Math is just what the Bad Old Math was—cookbookery. The difference is that the cookbooks are newer, more up to date—which may be a good thing, if cookbookery is what you want. Some of the cookbooks are not only newer, but better; but many, including some of the most highly touted, lavishly financed, and widely used, are not. Some I have examined are unclearly written; they contain many ambiguities; their examples are often ill chosen; they assume understandings that many children don't have; they do not make sufficiently strong the bridge between the known and real and the unknown and symbolic; they have too much material in them; they are too disconnected, too linear, too answer-directed. They are, in short, not worth all the fuss that is being made over them, and some of the children I know who are using them are as confused, baffled, and frightened as ever.

Children cannot learn much from cookbooks, even the best cookbooks. A child learns, at any

moment, not by using the procedure that seems
best to us, but the one that seems best to *him*; by
fitting into his structure of ideas and relationships,
his mental model of reality, not the piece we think
comes next, but the one he thinks comes next. This
is hard for teachers to learn, and hardest of all for
the skillful and articulate, the kind often called
"gifted." The more aware we are of the structural
nature of our own ideas, the more we are tempted
to try to transplant this structure whole into the
minds of children. But it cannot be done. They
must do this structuring and building for themselves. I may see that fact *A* and fact *B* are connected by a relationship *C*, but I can't make this
connection for a child by talking about it. He may
remember the facts and what I said about the relationship between them, but he is very likely to
turn my words into three facts, *A*, *B*, and *C*, none
of them connected to any other.

For example, consider that $2 \times 9 = 18$ and $2 \times 10 = 20$. Most children, and many teachers, see
these as unrelated facts; schools and textbooks are
used to talking about the 100 facts of multiplication. But these facts are joined by the relationship
that ten 2's must be 2 more than nine 2's. Knowing this, I know that 1000×2 must be 2 more
than 999×2, and thus I know, without having to
multiply, that 999×2 must equal $2000 - 2$, or
1998. But I have found, over and over again, when
I tried to point out this relationship to students,
that many of them took it in, if at all, only as a
third, rather complicated fact, that had nothing to
do with the others. A child must discover for
himself that if, for example, $2 \times 75 = 150$, then
2×74 must equal $150 - 2$, or 148. Until he does,

no amount of talk will enable him to make that step, far less make use of this understanding to see that since $3 \times 50 = 150$, 3×49 must equal $150 - 3$, or 147.

It has seemed to me for a long time that, though children are very good at inductive reasoning, at making generalizations from specific cases, they were poor at deductive reasoning, since even the best students could rarely give examples of any generalizations they happened to know. But the reason children can use so few of the generalizations they hear in school is that these generalizations are not theirs, and were never connected to reality in the first place. The kind of concrete math problems I have been describing gave children the chance to make generalizations, which though crude, were really their own, and therefore usable —a foundation on which they could build. But it was hard at first to see how to apply these problems, which I had used for diagnostic purposes, to the task of teaching the conventional arithmetic curriculum—numbers and operations with them. Then I saw the work of Professor Z. Dienes, a British mathematician and teacher, then working at Harvard, and new possibilities began to open up.

Professor Dienes has developed a way of teaching math that he calls the Math Laboratory. It was first used widely in the schools of Leicester County, England, and since then in many other places.

Children are given various kinds of materials, and a variety of experiments to do with them: to find how many of one piece are needed to make another, or how to use pieces of one shape to make another shape, and so forth. No one tells them how to do these things; they figure it out for themselves. If an experiment is too hard, they try an easier one. As they get their answers, they write them down. In time, they start to see that what they do at one time is rather like what they did at another. They begin to see similarities and make generalizations until, eventually, they can do certain problems without having to use the materials at all. Then they can be said to know the principle embodied in the problem.

These materials and experiments are most varied and ingenious. Children find them so interesting and such fun to work that, in the Leicestershire schools, one can often see a roomful of forty young children, even as young as seven years old, working intently each on his own experiment, sometimes with no teacher in the room at all. Some of these materials enable children to learn what few children know here—the meaning and use of base and place in a positional numeral system (ours is such a system, with a base of 10). Other Math Lab materials deal with quite different matters, including some that would be considered by most people much too difficult for the very children who have worked them with ease and pleasure.

There is no reason why, using these materials, the Cuisenaire rods, and other aids that mathematicians and ingenious teachers can invent, we could not teach all of arithmetic, and many other things besides, by the laboratory method. It will take time to find out what sort of materials are most interesting to children, and carry the most mathematical meaning; what sort of experiments can be done by children with the greatest pleasure and with the least possible instruction, inter-ference, and correction by the teacher. But such matters of detail and practice can easily be worked out by schools or teachers who understand the general method and the principles behind it—who are more interested in having children learn some-thing real than in having them get good marks on tests. In such schools, math might, in time, become one of the most popular and constructive courses instead of the most hated and harmful, a source of real and useful rather than apparent learning, a nourisher of thought and intelligence rather than a destroyer of them.

HOW SCHOOLS FAIL

February 27, 1958

A few days ago Nell came up to the desk, and looking at me steadily and without speaking, as usual, put on the desk her ink copy of the latest composition. Our rule is that on the ink copy there must be no more than three mistakes per page, or the page must be copied again. I checked her paper, and on the first page found five mistakes. I showed them to her, and told her, as gently as I could, that she had to copy it again, and urged her to be more careful—typical teacher's advice. She looked at me, heaved a sigh, and went back to her desk. She is left-handed, and doesn't manage a pen very well. I could see her frowning with concentration as she worked and struggled. Back she came after a while with the second copy. This time the first page had seven mistakes, and the handwriting was noticeably worse. I told her to copy it again. Another bigger sigh, and she went back to her desk. In time the third copy arrived, looking much worse than the second, and with even more mistakes.

At that point Bill Hull asked me a question, one I should have asked myself, one we ought all to keep asking ourselves: "Where are you trying to get, and are you getting there?"

The question sticks like a burr. In schools—but where isn't it so?—we so easily fall into the same trap: the means to an end becomes an end in itself. I had on my hands this three-mistake rule meant to serve the ends of careful work and neat compositions. By applying it rigidly was I getting more careful work and neater compositions? No; I was getting a child who was so worried about having to recopy her paper that she could not concentrate on doing it, and hence did it worse and worse, and would probably do the next papers badly as well.

We need to ask more often of everything we do in school, "Where are we trying to get, and is this thing we are doing helping us to get there?" Do we do something because we want to help the children and can see that what we are doing is helping them? Or do we do it because it is inexpensive or convenient for school, teachers, administrators? Or because everyone else does it? We must beware of making a virtue of necessity, and cooking up high-sounding educational reasons for doing what is done really for reasons of administrative economy or convenience. The still greater danger is that, having started to do something for good enough reasons, we may go on doing it stubbornly and blindly, as I did that day, unable or unwilling to see that we are doing more harm than good.

October 30, 1958

Everyone around here talks as if, except for a few hopeless characters, these children know most of the math they are supposed to know. It just isn't so. Out of the twenty kids in the class, there are at least six who don't even know simple "addition facts," and many more who, whether they know the facts or not, habitually add by counting on their fingers, usually keeping them well out of sight. There are still more who don't understand and can't do multiplication and division. I hate to think what we will find about their understanding of place value.

It would be easy to make up an arithmetic test that without being too long, or unfairly tricky, or covering anything but what these kids are supposed to know, would stump all but a few of the children in fifth grade. Or any grade. The ninth graders I taught came to me with respectable school records in arithmetic, yet they knew little about division, less about fractions, and next to nothing about decimals.

It begins to look as if the test-examination-marks business is a gigantic racket, the purpose of which is to enable students, teachers, and schools to take part in a joint pretense that the students know everything they are supposed to know, when in fact they know only a small part of it—if any at all. Why do we always announce exams in advance, if not to give students a chance to cram for them? Why do teachers, even in graduate schools, always say quite specifically what the exam will be about,

even telling the type of questions that will be
given? Because otherwise too many students
would flunk. What would happen at Harvard or
Yale if a prof gave a surprise test in March on
work covered in October? Everyone knows what
would happen; that's why they don't do it.

March 20, 1959

Today Jane did one of those things that, for all her
rebellious and annoying behavior in class, make
her one of the best and most appealing people,
young or old, that I have ever known. I was at the
board, trying to explain to her a point on long
division, when she said, in self-defense, "But Miss
W. (her fourth-grade teacher) told us that we
should take the first number . . ." Here she saw the
smallest shadow of doubt on my face. She knew
instantly that I did not approve of this rule, and
without so much as a pause she continued, ". . . it
wasn't Miss W., it was someone else . . ." and then
went on talking about long division.

I was touched and very moved. How many
adults would have seen what she saw, that what
she was saying about Miss W.'s teaching was, in
some slight degree, lowering my estimate of Miss
W.? Even more to the point, how many adults,
given this opportunity to shift the blame for their
difficulties onto the absent Miss W., would instead
have instantly changed their story to protect her
from blame? For all our yammering about loyalty,
not one adult in a thousand would have shown the
loyalty that this little girl gave to her friend and
former teacher. And she scarcely had to think to

do it; for her, to defend one's friends from harm, blame, or even criticism was an instinct as natural as breathing.

Teachers and schools tend to mistake good behavior for good character. What they prize above all else is docility, suggestibility; the child who will do what he is told; or even better, the child who will do what is wanted without even having to be told. They value most in children what children least value in themselves. Small wonder that their effort to build character is such a failure; they don't know it when they see it. Jane is a good example. She has been a trial to everyone who has taught her. Even this fairly lenient school finds her barely tolerable; most schools long since would have kicked her out in disgrace. Of the many adults who have known her, probably very few have recognized her extraordinary qualities or appreciated their worth. Asked for an estimate of her character, most of them would probably say that it was bad. Yet, troublesome as she is, I wish that there were more children like her.

April 11, 1959

The things children talk about in class, when they are allowed to talk at all, are seldom close to their hearts. Only once in a great while do I feel, at the end of a class discussion, that I have come close to the real life of these children. One such discussion was about hiding places; another, just a few days ago, was about names.

This latter came up in Roman history. The time arrived in Rome when the mob gained political power, so that the ability to arouse and inflame the mob was a sure key to high office. The kids wanted to know how this was done. I said it was done mostly with names. The way to arouse a mob against your political opponent was to call him names, the kind of names the mob hates most, or can be talked into hating. The mob spirit is weaker in these children than it will be in a few years, and they were skeptical; they wanted to know what kind of names would arouse a mob.

For answer, I asked them, "Well, what kind of names do you hate to be called?" We were off. Before the end of the period the board was covered with names. About half were what I expected, the usual ten-year-old insults—idiot, stupid, nuthead, fat slob, chicken, dope, scaredy-cat, etc. The rest surprised me. They were all terms of endearment.

It was quite a scene. There were all these bright-faced, lively children, eyes dancing with excitement and enthusiasm, seeing who could most strongly express their collective contempt and disgust for all the names that adults might suppose they like most. Someone would say, "Dearie—ug-g-g-g-gh!" Chorus of agreement. Someone else would say, "Honey—ic-c-c-c-ch!" More agreement. Every imaginable term of affection and endearment came in for its share. Not one was legitimate, not one was accepted. Nobody said of any term, "Well, that's not too bad." To some extent the children may have been carried away by the excitement of the game, but from the way they looked and sounded I felt sure, and do now, that they really meant what they were saying, that their dislike of these terms of endearment was genuine and deeply felt.

Why should this be? Of course, ten is a heroic age for most kids. They remind me in many ways of the Homeric Greeks. They are quarrelsome and combative; they have a strong and touchy sense of honor; they believe that every affront must be repaid, and with interest; they are fiercely loyal to their friends, even though they may change friends often; they have little sense of fair play, and greatly admire cunning and trickery; they are both highly possessive and very generous—no smallest trifle may be taken from them, but they are likely to give anything away, if they feel so disposed. Most of the time, they don't feel like little children, and they don't like being talked to as if they were little children.

But there is more to it than this. They suspect and resent these terms of endearment because they have too often heard them used by people who did not mean them. Everyone who deals with children these days has heard the dictum that children need to be loved, must be loved. But even to those who like them most, children are not always a joy and delight to be with. Often they are much like older people, and often they are exasperating and irritating. It is not surprising that there are many adults who do not like children much, if at all. But they feel that they ought to like them, have a duty to like them, and they try to discharge this duty by acting, particularly by talking, as if they liked them. Hence the continual and meaningless use of words like *honey, dearie,* etc. Hence, the dreadful, syrupy voice that so many adults use when they speak to children. By the time they are ten, children are fed up with this fake affection, and ready to believe that, most of the time, adults believe and mean very little of what they say.

May 3, 1959

The more I see of our troublemaking Jane, and the more I think about her, the clearer it becomes that she has a great need to feel truly loved, but feels that being loved when she is nice, good, obedient, etc. does not count. *Loved* is a tricky word here; perhaps I should say admired, appreciated, or even honored and respected. She is like Cyrano; she thinks nothing could be more contemptible than to try to get approval and affection from others by saying, doing, and being what they want.

Isn't there much to admire in this? Perhaps someday she will feel that she can oblige and help the people she likes without having to worry about whether she gets anything out of it for herself. Right now, she finds it hard to show her natural affection, as other children might, just by being affectionate. On the contrary, she feels she must continually test, by misbehaving, the affection of others for her. Now and then she miscalculates, and draws down on herself a punishment that she thinks is too severe, and so falls into a cycle of angry rebellion that she does not know how to break.

She is at my lunch table these days, and is delightful company; she's even making vague gestures in the direction of better table manners. I wish I could persuade her that she need not every day give our affection for her the acid test, but I guess only time will do that. At lunch the other day she said to me, "I *hate* teachers!" and then gave me a 1/100th-of-a-second smile and a hard sock on the arm. How much easier her life would be if we did not continually oblige her to choose between our adult approval and her own self-respect.

June 3, 1959

I've corrected and scored the final math tests. The results are not quite as dismal as last week; most people did a little better. But one exception suggests that drill is not always as helpful as most people think. Caroline took the first test after being out two weeks, during which she missed much review work. She surprised me by getting 15 out of 25. Today, after taking the other test a week ago, and after a week of further review, she got only 7 right. It looks as if she learns more when she is out of school than when she is in it.

Looking at the low gang, I feel angry and disgusted with myself for having given these tests. The good students didn't need them; the poor students, during this month or more of preparation and review, had most of whatever confidence and common sense they had picked up during the year knocked right out of them. Looking at Monica today, on the edge of tears, unable to bring herself even to try most of the problems, I felt that I had literally done her an injury.

There was a lot of room for improvement in the rather loose classes I was running last fall, but the children were doing some real thinking and learning, and were gaining confidence in their own powers. From a blind *producer* Ben was on his way to being a very solid and imaginative *thinker;* now he has fallen back into recipe-following production strategy of the worst kind. What is this test nonsense, anyway? Do people go through life taking math tests, with other people telling them to hurry? Are we trying to turn out intelligent people, or test-takers?

There must be a way to educate young children so that the great human qualities that we know are in them may be developed. But we'll never do it as long as we are obsessed with tests. At faculty meetings we talk about how to reward the *thinkers* in our classes. Who is kidding whom? No amount of rewards and satisfactions obtained in the small group thinking sessions will make up to Monica for what she felt today, faced by a final test that she knew she couldn't do and was going to fail. Pleasant experiences don't make up for painful ones. No child, once painfully burned, would agree to be burned again, however enticing the reward. For all our talk and good intentions, there is much more stick than carrot in school, and while this remains so, children are going to adopt a strategy aimed above all else at staying out of trouble. How can we foster a joyous, alert, whole-hearted participation in life, if we build all our schooling around the holiness of getting "right answers?"

March 8, 1960

The other day a lady said for me, better than I ever could have said it for myself, just what is wrong with the whole school setup. During this past vacation I visited a school that was still in session. It has the reputation of being very "good" and "tough." The headmistress, who was very nice, asked me where I had taught. When I told her, she said with false humility, "I'm afraid you'll find us very old-fashioned." But she made me welcome, and particularly urged me to visit the arithmetic class of her fourth-grade teacher, who had been there for many years and was generally felt to be a jewel among teachers and the pride of the school. I went. Soon after I arrived the class began. The children had done some multiplication problems and, in turn, were reading answers from their marked papers. All went smoothly until, right after a child had read his answer, another child raised his hand. "What is it, Jimmy?" the teacher asked, with just the faintest hint in her voice that this interruption could not be really necessary. "Well, I didn't get that answer," said Jimmy, "I got . . ." but before he could say more, the teacher said, "Now, Jimmy, I'm sure we don't want to hear any *wrong* answers." And that was the last word out of Jimmy.

This woman is far ahead of most teachers in intelligence, education, and experience. She is articulate, cultivated, has had a good schooling, and is married to a college professor. And in the twenty years or more that she has been teaching it has apparently never occurred to her that it might be worth taking a moment now and then to hear these unsuccessful Jimmies talk about their wrong answers, on the chance that from their talk she might learn something about their thinking and what was making the answers come out wrong. What makes everyone call her such a good teacher? I suppose it is the ability to manage children effortlessly, which she does. And for all I know, even the Jimmies may think she is a good teacher; it would never occur to them that it was this nice lady's fault that they couldn't understand arithmetic; no, it must be their own fault, for being so stupid.

April 17, 1960

Here are first graders, learning to read by the supposedly well-worked-out and highly regarded Gillingham method. The method requires that they be able to say which letters are vowels and which are consonants. Instead of telling them sensibly that we call a few letters vowels and the others consonants, the method tries to have them learn the difference by definition—always a bad way, even when the definition is good. So the teacher tells them, "A consonant is a cut-off sound, made without using the vocal chords." They will be required to learn this definition, repeat it from memory, and give examples of it. They look confused, but their confusions have just begun, because this definition, though true of many consonants, is not true of many others, like *z*, the *g* of George, *l*, *r*, *m*, *n*, and *v*; and is only half-true of still others, like *s*, *f*, *sh*, *ch*, etc. Eventually the children will learn that some letters are called vowels because that is what we decided to call them, but this false definition of consonant is going to give them much trouble in the meantime.

Why do we tell children things that about one

minute's thought would tell us are not true? Partly because we ourselves do not need the definition to know what a vowel is, and hence are not troubled by its inconsistency. I know a dog, or a vowel, when I see one, so I don't care how you define them. Also, like many children, we are apt to follow rules blindly, without thinking about them or checking them against fact. But the main reason we are careless about what we say to children is that we think it doesn't make any difference. We underestimate their intellectual ability, the extent to which (at least at first) they think about what they hear, try to make sense out of it, and are baffled, upset, and frightened when they cannot.

Children so taught do very odd things. One boy, quite a good student, was working on the problem, "If you have 6 jugs, and you want to put ⅔ of a pint of lemonade into each jug, how much lemonade will you need?" His answer was 18 pints. I said, "How much in each jug?" "Two-thirds of a pint." I said, "Is that more or less than a pint?" "Less." I said, "How many jugs are there?" "Six." I said, "But that doesn't make any sense." He shrugged his shoulders and said, "Well, that's the way the system worked out." Precisely. He has long since quit expecting school to make sense. They tell you these facts and rules, and your job is to put them down on paper the way they tell you. Never mind whether they mean anything or not.

That reminds me. In a number of first-grade classes I have seen tacked up on the wall a notice saying, "When two vowels go out walking, the first one does the talking." Very nice. A little further inspection shows that in that sentence there are two pairs of vowels, both of which violate the rule. Now what are children expected to make of this?

I told some friends about the lemonade boy, to show why I objected to so much of our teaching. They felt he must be unusual, that most children find school sensible and connected with life. Not ten minutes later, in the backyard, I had this conversation with their daughter, then in second grade.

"How's school these days?"

"OK."

"What sort of stuff do they teach you?" (I hardly ever ask this question any more.)

Pause. "Oh, stuff like the difference between 'gone' and 'went.'"

"I see. By the way, can you tell me which is right, 'I have gone to the movies' or 'I have went to the movies.'"

Long, thoughtful pause. Then, "I don't know; I can't tell when it isn't written on the board."

We both laughed at this.

Later, swearing them to secrecy (I knew I could trust them), I told the child's parents this story. They said ruefully that they began to see what I meant.

Second graders, who had supposedly been taught "phonics" by the Gillingham method, were asked by their teacher, "What letter does Potomac begin with?" There was a chorus of guesses—*P, T, V,* and many others—with the children all trying to get clues from each other and the teacher. A few children really knew, and their conviction, as well as their reputation for usually being right in such matters, won over the others, so that after a while they were all saying *P.* And the teacher looked pleased and satisfied! Later, pointing to a map on the wall, she asked, "Which way would you go if you flew east?" Arms waved in all directions, again settling down as everyone got his cue from the successful student and the teacher's encouraging expressions.

Later, in music class, the children were asked to touch their toes when the teacher played a *C*. The teacher then played a little march, to which the children walked around. Every time she came to a *C*, she held it. Naturally, the children touched their toes each time. Just as naturally, they touched them if any note other than *C* was held, and when *C* was played without being held, they ignored it. And this woman thought she was teaching them *C!* And she has been doing this now for ten or maybe twenty years—and in one of our "best" schools.

Children in the *right-wrong* situation will naturally grasp at every available clue. We teachers have to learn to present problems so that irrelevant clues will not lead so often to correct performance. We must learn to know when our faces and minds are being read, and to mix our signals accordingly. Even more important, we must make children more aware of their own strategies, the ways in which they try to get us to do their thinking for them. I often say to kids, supposedly working on a problem, "Why are you staring at me; the answer isn't going to appear on my forehead." Made aware of what they were doing, they usually laughed. It would be better yet, I suppose, to turn away so that they couldn't see my face at all.

When a child gets right answers by illegitimate means, and gets credit for knowing what he doesn't know, and knows he doesn't know, it does double harm. First, he doesn't learn, his confusions are not cleared up; secondly, he comes to believe that a combination of bluffing, guessing, mind reading, snatching at clues, and getting answers from other people is what he is supposed to do at school; that this is what school is all about; that nothing else is possible.

April 22, 1960

Trudy had to add $20 + 7$. She counted it out on her fingers. I thought, "What now?" I keep thinking I have plumbed the bottom of these children's ignorance, and I am always wrong. On a fresh sheet of paper I wrote $10 + 3 =$. She counted on her fingers and got 13. I wrote it down. Right under this problem I wrote $10 + 9 =$. When she got 19, I wrote it down. In turn, I gave her $10 + 4$, $10 + 5$, $10 + 3$, $10 + 6$, $10 + 2$. Each time she counted on her fingers to get the answer. Then I gave her $10 + 6$ a second time. She counted on her fingers, said 16, and then looked at the paper for a bit. Then she said, "Mr. Holt, there's always a 1 and then the same number you added." A discovery! I was very pleased and said, "Let's see, yes, you're right." I then gave her more of the same problems, and also $20 + 5$, $20 + 9$, $20 + 6$, $40 + 3$, and so on. She did all of them without counting on her fingers.

After I got over feeling pleased with myself and her, I had second thoughts. Had she really learned anything that she could or would use in other contexts? Did she think it was reasonable that numerals should act this way? Or was it just another mysterious coincidence? Did it make sense, or was it just another recipe, one more thing to remember, one more thing that would trip her up if she forgot it? If she felt that way, she would probably go back to finger-counting, which she feels is at least reliable. And go back she did, in less than a week.

I suppose this child has been told a thousand times, maybe two thousand, that when you add a number to 10 you get your answer by writing a 1 and then the number you added, yet when she discovered it the other day it was as if she had never seen it before. What on earth would be the use of my telling her again? When you show a child ten times over how to do something, and he still can't do it, you might as well stop. You're not making any connection with whatever is inside his head. You must go at the matter another way.

One day I asked Trudy to write out her 7 tables. She counted on her fingers to get each answer—even for 7×2. She has been told umpteen times that $7 \times 2 = 14$, and has written it many times. Perhaps she even knows it, in the sense that if I said to her, "What is 7×2?" she could answer, "14." But it is not a piece of knowledge that she dares rely on in a pinch—safer to use those fingers. Counting, she got up to $6 \times 7 = 42$ without a slip. Then she made the kind of mistake that children tend to make when they are bored. She wrote $8 \times 7 = 49$. Naturally, there was no self-checker to say "Whoa, wait a minute, that doesn't look right." Then she wrote $9 \times 7 = 56$; but she made the 6 rather badly, so that it looked like a zero, which is how she read it. This gave her $10 \times 7 =$

57, 11 × 7 = 64, 12 × 7 = 71. And there was not a flicker of doubt or hesitation as she wrote down these absurdities. She was counting on her fingers, and carefully, wasn't she? So how *could* she make a mistake?

I took the paper away and asked her to write the 7 table again. This time I got 7, 14, 21, 28, 36, 43, 50, 57, 64, 71, 78, 85.

I took this paper away and asked her to do it again. This time, after a slip that I pointed out and she corrected, she gave me a correct set of answers.

Then I had what seemed at the time like a bright idea. I thought if I could get her to think about what she had written, she would see that some of her answers were more reasonable than others, and thus the beginnings of an error-noticing, nonsense-eliminating device might take root in her mind. I gave her all three papers, and asked her, since they did not agree, to compare her answers, check with a √ those she felt sure were right, with an X those she felt sure were wrong, and with a *?* those she wasn't sure of one way or the other.

A moment later I got one of the most unpleasant surprises of my teaching career. She handed me her correct paper, with 7 × 1 marked right, and *all other answers* marked wrong.

This poor child has been defeated and destroyed by school. Years of drill, practice, explanation, and testing—the whole process we call education—have done nothing for her except help to knock her loose from what common sense she might have had to start with. What else has she to show for five years worth of struggling and suffering over arithmetic? What kind of an adult is she going to grow up to be? How is she ever going to be able to make any sense of the world she will have to live in? What kind of fortresses of delusion and false security is she going to build for herself in her mind?

It is hard not to feel that in every way it would have been much better for her never to have had to study arithmetic at all. All it has done for her is make school a place of pain and danger, where she is so busy thinking about escape and safety that she can learn almost nothing, and use nothing of what she learns.

April 27, 1960

We teachers, from primary school through graduate school, all seem to be hard at work at the business of making it look as if our students know more than they really do. Our standing among other teachers, or of our school among other schools, depends on how much our students seem to know; not on how much they really know, or how effectively they can use what they know, or even whether they can use it at all. The more material we can appear to "cover" in our course, or syllabus, or curriculum, the better we look; and the more easily we can show that when they left our class our students knew what they were "supposed" to know, the more easily can we escape blame if and when it later appears (and it usually does) that much of that material they do not know at all.

When I was in my last year at school, we seniors stayed around an extra week to cram for college boards. Our ancient history teacher told us, on the basis of long experience, that we would do well to prepare ourselves to write for twenty minutes on each of a list of fifteen topics that he gave us. We studied his list. We knew the wisdom of taking that kind of advice; if we had not, we would not have been at that school. When the boards came, we found that his list comfortably covered every one of the eight questions we were asked. So we got credit for knowing a great deal about ancient history, which we did not, he got credit for being a good teacher, which he was not, and the school got credit for being, as it was, a good place to go if you wanted to be sure of getting into a prestige college. The fact was that I knew very little about ancient history; that much of what I thought I knew was misleading or false; that then, and for many years afterwards, I disliked history and thought it pointless and a waste of time; and that two months later I could not have come close to passing the history college boards, or even a much easier test. But who cared?

I have played the game myself. When I began teaching I thought, naïvely, that the purpose of a test was to test, to find out what the students knew about the course. It didn't take me long to find out that if I gave my students surprise tests, covering the whole material of the course to date, almost everyone flunked. This made me look bad, and posed problems for the school. I learned that the only way to get a respectable percentage of decent or even passing grades was to announce tests well in advance, tell in some detail what material they would cover, and hold plenty of advance practice in the kind of questions that would be asked, which is called review. I later learned that teachers do this everywhere. We know that what we are doing is not really honest, but we dare not be the first to stop, and we try to justify or excuse ourselves by saying that, after all, it does no particular harm. But we are wrong; it does great harm.

It does harm, first of all, because it is dishonest and the students know it. My friends and I, breezing through the ancient history Boards, knew very well that a trick was being played on someone, we were not quite sure on whom. Our success on the Boards was due, not to our knowledge of ancient history, which was scanty, but to our teacher's skill as a predicter, which was great. Even children much younger than we were learn that what most teachers want and reward are not knowledge and understanding but the appearance of them. The smart and able ones, at least, come to look on school as something of a racket, which it is their job to learn how to beat. And learn they do; they become experts at smelling out the unspoken and often unconscious preferences and prejudices of their teachers, and at taking full advantage of them. My first English teacher at prep school gave us Macaulay's *Essay on Lord Clive* to read, and from his pleasure in reading it aloud, I saw that he was a sucker for the periodic sentence, a long complex sentence with the main verb at the end. Thereafter I took care to construct at least one such sentence in every paper I wrote for him, and thus assured myself a good mark in the course.

Not only does the examination racket do harm by making students feel that a search for honest understanding is beside the point; it does further harm by discouraging those few students who go on making that search in spite of everything. The student who will not be satisfied merely to know "right answers" or recipes for getting them will not have an easy time in school, particularly since facts and recipes may be all that his teachers know. They tend to be impatient or even angry with the student who wants to know, not just what happened, but why it happened as it did, and not some other way. They rarely have the knowledge to answer such questions, and even more rarely have the time; there is all that material to cover.

In short, our "Tell-'em-and-test-'em" way of teaching leaves most students increasingly confused, aware that their academic success rests on shaky foundations, and convinced that school is mainly a place where you follow meaningless procedures to get meaningless answers to meaningless questions.

July 10, 1960

Two arguments are put forward in favor of tests. One is that the threat of the test makes children work harder, and therefore better. The other is that the test tells the teacher how much the children have actually learned. Both arguments are false. To the extent that children really feel threatened by tests, they work worse, not better. And tests do not show what children have learned. Not only do they fail to show how much many able children do know, but they fail to do what one might have expected them to do—expose the child who knows nothing at all.

One day I was working with Trudy and Eleanor who is, if anything, even a poorer student with even less of an idea about how numbers work. On the board I wrote:

$$256$$
$$+\ \underline{327}$$

I then did the problem, step by step, slowly, doing every step aloud, and giving them plenty of time to think about what I was doing, until I got the answer, 583, which I wrote. Then, beside the old problem, I wrote a new one, so that we had on the board

$$256 \qquad\qquad 256$$
$$+\ \underline{327} \qquad\qquad +\ \underline{328}$$
$$583$$

I said, "We're going to add something to 256 again, but this time, instead of adding 327, we are to add 328. This time, you do it." Would they see that the answer had to be 1 larger than the first answer, or 584? No; after working together on the problem for a while, on paper, they said tentatively, "353?"

I then wrote a new problem, and did it aloud, step by step, until they were satisfied it was correct. Then right beside it I wrote exactly the same problem, so that we had on the board

$$245 \qquad\qquad 245$$
$$+\ \underline{179} \qquad\quad +\ \underline{179}$$
$$424$$

I asked them to do the second problem. They did not see that it was the same, and bent once more over the paper. After much writing, they said, "524."

I did this again, using the problem $88 + 94 = 182$; but this time they saw, though only after some time, that it was the same problem, and must have the same answer.

A short time later I wrote $2 \times 12 = 24$; $2 \times 13 = $. Eleanor promptly said, "I can't read it that way," but after I had written it the way she was used to, went to work and in time gave me the correct answer, 26. Trudy gave me 68. She read the thoughts on my face, and said hastily, "Wait a minute." After a while she wrote 36. I said, "How did you get it?" She went to the board, and wrote $2 \times 12 = 24$, $3 \times 12 = $. She did not even notice that she had changed the problem. Then she said, "Well, there'd be one more." Then she wrote $2 + 1 = 3$, $4 + 1 = 5$, and then the answer, 35, saying "Is that right?"

Not long afterward Eleanor told me that $20 + 10 = 29$.

These children, like almost all children in elementary school, take once or twice every year a series of tests misnamed Achievement Tests. There are several varieties of these, all very much alike and equally worthless. In theory they enable teachers and schools to measure the "achievement" (what a word to describe what children spend most of their time doing in school!) of their pupils against that of pupils of similar age all over the country. In fact they encourage a kind of cheating; teachers are not supposed to cram children for these tests, but most of them do, particularly in schools that make a fetish of high test scores—which they call "high standards."

The tests are designed so that a child's score comes out as a grade equivalent. The average fifth grader should score about 5.5 on most of his tests, and such a score would show that a child was about equal in achievement to an average fifth grader. The confused and hopeless children that I have worked with naturally never test as well as their abler classmates; but they are never much more than a year or two behind. This year, according to the tests, my worst pupils had the mathematical knowledge and skill of an average child entering fourth grade. In short, they presumably knew addition, subtraction, place value, multiplication, and easy division. But this is utter nonsense. These children know *nothing* about arithmetic; in any *real* sense they don't know what first graders are supposed to know. An accurate test, if there could be such a thing, a measuring instrument that really measured something, would give them a score of one point something.

How are these high scores achieved? A week or two before the tests, their teachers begin an intensive drilling on all the kinds of problems they will have to do on the test. By the time the test comes along the children are conditioned, like Pavlov's dog; when they see a certain arrangement of numerals and symbols before them, lights begin to flash, wheels begin to turn, and like robots they go through the answer-getting process, or enough of them to get a halfway decent score. Teachers are not supposed to do this; but they all do. So did I. The school asked me to, rather apologetically, knowing my feelings in such matters, but firmly nonetheless; when children pull down bad test scores there is an instant uproar from the parents. And it makes it hard for the kids when the time comes for them to enter their next schools. Schools being what they are, these poor devils are going to have trouble enough as it is; why make it harder for them by making their abysmal ignorance a matter of public record? So I go along with the practice. But is this a sensible way to carry out the education of our children?

· *December 4, 1960*

Some time ago, in an article on race stereotypes, I read something that stuck in my mind, but that only recently has seemed to have anything to do with children.

The author spent some time in a German concentration camp during the war. He and his fellow prisoners, trying to save both their lives and something of their human dignity, and to resist, despite their impotence, the demands of their jailers, evolved a kind of camp personality as a way of dealing with them. They adopted an air of amiable dullwittedness, of smiling foolishness, of cooperative and willing incompetence—like the good soldier Schweik. Told to do something, they listened attentively, nodded their heads eagerly, and asked questions that showed they had not understood a word of what had been said. When they could not safely do this any longer, they did as far as possible the opposite of what they had been told to do, or did it, but as badly as they dared. They realized that this did not much impede the German war effort, or even the administration of the camp; but it gave them a way of preserving a small part of their integrity in a hopeless situation.

After the war, the author did a good deal of work, in many parts of the world, with subject peoples; but not for some time did he recognize, in the personality of the "good black boy" of many African colonies, or the "good nigger" of the American South, the camp personality adopted during the war by himself and his fellow prisoners. When he first saw the resemblance, he was startled. Did these people, as he had done, put on this personality deliberately? He became convinced that this was true. Subject peoples both appease their rulers and satisfy some part of their desire for human dignity by putting on a mask, by acting much more stupid and incompetent than they really are, by denying their rulers the full use of their intelligence and ability, by declaring their minds and spirits free of their enslaved bodies.

Does not something very close to this happen often in school? Children are subject peoples. School for them is a kind of jail. Do they not, to some extent, escape and frustrate the relentless, insatiable pressure of their elders by withdrawing the most intelligent and creative parts of their minds from the scene? Is this not at least a partial explanation of the extraordinary stupidity that otherwise bright children so often show in school? The stubborn and dogged "I don't get it" with which they meet the instructions and explanations of their teachers—may it not be a statement of resistance as well as one of panic and flight?

I think this is almost certainly so. Whether children do this consciously and deliberately depends on the age and character of the child. Under pressure that they want to resist but don't dare to resist openly, some children may quite deliberately *go stupid;* I have seen it and felt it. Most of them, however, are probably not this aware of what they are doing. They deny their intelligence to their jailers, the teachers, not so much to frustrate them but because they have other and more important uses for it. Freedom to live and to think about life for its own sake is important and even essential to a child. He will only give so much time and thought to what others want him to do; the rest he demands and takes for his own interests, plans, worries, dreams. The result is that he is not all there during most of his hours in school. Whether he is afraid to be there, or just does not want to be there, the result is the same. Fear, boredom, resistance—they all go to make what we call stupid children.

To a very great degree, school is a place where children learn to be stupid. A dismal thought, but hard to escape. Infants are not stupid. Children of one, two, or even three throw the whole of themselves into everything they do. They embrace life, and devour it; it is why they learn so fast, and are such good company. Listlessness, boredom, apathy —these all come later. Children come to school *curious;* within a few years most of that curiosity is dead, or at least silent. Open a first or third grade to questions, and you will be deluged; fifth graders say nothing. They either have no questions or will not ask them. They think, "What's this leading up to? What's the catch?" Last year, thinking that self-consciousness and embarrassment might be silencing the children, I put a question box in the classroom, and said that I would answer any questions they put into it. In four months I got one question —"How long does a bear live?" While I was talking about the life span of bears and other creatures, one child said impatiently, "Come on, get to the point." The expressions on the children's faces seemed to say, "You've got us here in school; now make us do whatever it is that you want us to do." Curiosity, questions, speculation—these are for outside school, not inside.

Boredom and resistance may cause as much stupidity in school as fear. Give a child the kind of task he gets in school, and whether he is afraid of it, or resists it, or is willing to do it but bored by it, he will do the task with only a small part of his attention, energy, and intelligence. In a word, he will do it stupidly—even if correctly. This soon becomes a habit. He gets used to working at low power, he develops strategies to enable him to get by this way. In time he even starts to think of himself as being stupid, which is what most fifth graders think of themselves, and to think that his low-power way of coping with school is the only possible way.

It does no good to tell such students to pay attention and think about what they are doing. I can see myself now, in one of my ninth-grade algebra classes in Colorado, looking at one of my flunking students, a boy who had become frozen in his school stupidity, and saying to him in a loud voice,

"Think! Think! Think!" Wasted breath; he had forgotten how. The stupid way—timid, unimaginative, defensive, evasive—in which he met and dealt with the problems of algebra were, by that time, the only way he knew of dealing with them. His strategies and expectations were fixed; he couldn't even imagine any others. He really was doing his dreadful best.

We ask children to do for most of a day what few adults are able to do even for an hour. How many of us, attending, say, a lecture that doesn't interest us, can keep our minds from wandering? Hardly any. Not I, certainly. Yet children have far less awareness of and control of their attention than we do. No use to shout at them to pay attention. If we want to get tough enough about it, as many schools do, we can terrorize a class of children into sitting still with their hands folded and their eyes glued on us, or somebody; but their minds will be far away. The attention of children must be lured, caught, and held, like a shy wild animal that must be coaxed with bait to come close. If the situations, the materials, the problems before a child do not interest him, his attention will slip off to what does interest him, and no amount of exhortation or threats will bring it back.

A child is most intelligent when the reality before him arouses in him a high degree of attention, interest, concentration, involvement—in short, when he cares most about what he is doing. This is why we should make schoolrooms and schoolwork as interesting and exciting as possible, not just so that school will be a pleasant place, but so that children in school will act intelligently and get into *the habit* of acting intelligently. The case against boredom in school is the same as the case against fear; it makes children behave stupidly, some on purpose, most because they cannot help it. If this goes on long enough, as it does in school, they forget what it is like to grasp at something, as they once grasped at everything, with all their minds and senses; they forget how to deal positively and aggressively with life and experience, to think and say, "I see it! I get it! I can do it!"

April 9, 1961

The section on Real Learning described some of the non-symbolic work that Marjorie did with Cuisenaire rods. But words cannot describe the freedom, the happiness, the lack of tension, the alertness, the concentration, the intellectual power that she showed doing this work. She was like someone I had never seen before. For most of her years in school she has been cheating or bluffing, using illegitimate tactics to pry right answers out of other people, and pretending to know and understand what she did not. Now she was free of the need for all this.

When I hear in my mind her voice saying, "It's such fun when you get the trick," it makes me sad, and angry, and appalled, that in our well-meaning way we have given this child, and many others, so few opportunities for real thought and discovery, honest understanding. We have done to their intelligence what denying them good food would have done to their bodies. We have made them intellectually weak and stunted, and worse, dishonest. No doubt children are clever about fooling their teachers about what they know; but the job is made much easier by the fact that we, their teachers, are so ready, so eager to be fooled, to tell ourselves that children know what a few minutes careful inspection would show they did not know at all.

June 15, 1961

A mother said to me not long ago, "I think you are making a mistake in trying to make schoolwork so interesting for the children. After all, they are going to have to spend most of their lives doing things they don't like, and they might as well get used to it now."

Every so often the curtain of slogans and platitudes behind which most people live opens up for a second, and you get a glimpse of what they really think. This is not the first time a parent has said this to me, but it horrifies me as much as ever. What an extraordinary view of life, from one of the favored citizens of this most favored of all nations! Is life nothing but drudgery, an endless list of dreary duties? Is education nothing but the process of getting children ready to do them? It was as if she had said, "My boy is going to have to spend his life as a slave, so I want you to get him used to the idea, and see to it that when he gets to be a slave, he will be a dutiful and diligent and well paid one."

It's easy to see how an adult, in a discouraged moment, hemmed in by seemingly pointless and petty duties and responsibilities, might think of life as a kind of slavery. But one would expect that people feeling this way about their own lives would want something better for their children, would say, in effect, "I have somehow missed the chance to put much joy and meaning into my own life; please educate my children so that they will do better."

Well, that's our business, whether parents say it or not.

This woman is attractive, intelligent, fond of her son, and interested in him. Yet she shares with many parents and teachers a belief about her child and children in general which is both profoundly disrespectful and untrue. It is that they never do anything and never will do anything "worthwhile" unless some adult makes them do it. All this woman's stories about herself and her boy have the same plot: at first, he doesn't want to do something; then, she makes him do it; finally, he does it well, and maybe even enjoys it. She never tells me stories about things that her boy does well without being made to, and she seems uninterested and even irritated when I tell her such stories. The only triumphs of his that she savors are those for which she can give herself most of the credit.

Children sense this attitude. They resent it, and they are right to resent it. By what right do we assume that there is nothing good in children except what we put there? This view is condescending and presumptuous. More important, it is untrue, and blinds us to the fact that in our clumsy and ignorant efforts to mold the character of children we probably destroy at least as many good qualities as we develop, do at least as much harm as good.

TO SUMMARIZE

When we talk about intelligence, we do not mean the ability to get a good score on a certain kind of test, or even the ability to do well in school; these are at best only indicators of something larger, deeper, and far more important. By intelligence we mean a style of life, a way of behaving in various situations, and particularly in new, strange, and perplexing situations. The true test of intelligence is not how much we know how to do, but how we behave when we don't know what to do.

The intelligent person, young or old, meeting a new situation or problem, opens himself up to it; he tries to take in with mind and senses everything he can about it; he thinks about *it*, instead of about himself or what it might cause to happen to him; he grapples with it boldly, imaginatively, resourcefully, and if not confidently at least hopefully; if he fails to master it, he looks without shame or fear at his mistakes and learns what he can from them. This is intelligence. Clearly its roots lie in a certain feeling about life, and one's self with respect to life. Just as clearly, unintelligence is not what most psychologists seem to suppose, the same thing as intelligence only less of it. It is an entirely different style of behavior, arising out of an entirely different set of attitudes.

Years of watching and comparing bright children and the not-bright, or less bright, have shown that they are very different kinds of people. The bright child is curious about life and reality, eager to get in touch with it, embrace it, unite himself with it. There is no wall, no barrier between him and life. The dull child is far less curious, far less interested in what goes on and what is real, more inclined to live in worlds of fantasy. The bright child likes to experiment, to try things out. He lives by the maxim that there is more than one way to skin a cat. If he can't do something one way, he'll try another. The dull child is usually afraid to try at all. It takes a good deal of urging to get him to try even once; if that try fails, he is through.

The bright child is patient. He can tolerate uncertainty and failure, and will keep trying until he gets an answer. When all his experiments fail, he can even admit to himself and others that for the time being he is not going to get an answer. This may annoy him, but he can wait. Very often, he does not want to be told how to do the problem or solve the puzzle he has struggled with, because he does not want to be cheated out of the chance to figure it out for himself in the future. Not so the dull child. He cannot stand uncertainty or failure. To him, an unanswered question is not a challenge or an opportunity, but a threat. If he can't find the answer quickly, it must be given to him, and quickly; and he must have answers for everything. Such are the children of whom a second-grade teacher once said, "But my children *like* to have

questions for which there is only one answer."
They did; and by a mysterious coincidence, so did she.

The bright child is willing to go ahead on the basis of incomplete understanding and information. He will take risks, sail uncharted seas, explore when the landscape is dim, the landmarks few, the light poor. To give only one example, he will often read books he does not understand in the hope that after a while enough understanding will emerge to make it worth while to go on. In this spirit some of my fifth graders tried to read *Moby Dick*. But the dull child will go ahead only when he thinks he knows exactly where he stands and exactly what is ahead of him. If he does not feel he knows exactly what an experience will be like, and if it will not be exactly like other experiences he already knows, he wants no part of it. For while the bright child feels that the universe is, on the whole, a sensible, reasonable, and trustworthy place, the dull child feels that it is senseless, unpredictable, and treacherous. He feels that he can never tell what may happen, particularly in a new situation, except that it will probably be bad.

Nobody starts off stupid. You have only to watch babies and infants, and think seriously about what all of them learn and do, to see that, except for the most grossly retarded, they show a style of life, and a desire and ability to learn that in an older person we might well call genius. Hardly an adult in a thousand, or ten thousand, could in any three years of his life learn as much, grow as much in his understanding of the world around him, as every infant learns and grows in his first three years. But what happens, as we get older, to this extraordinary capacity for learning and intellectual growth?

What happens is that it is destroyed, and more than by any other one thing, by the process that we misname education—a process that goes on in most homes and schools. We adults destroy most of the intellectual and creative capacity of children by the things we do to them or make them do. We destroy this capacity above all by making them afraid, afraid of not doing what other people want, of not pleasing, of making mistakes, of failing, of being *wrong*. Thus we make them afraid to gamble, afraid to experiment, afraid to try the difficult and the unknown. Even when we do not create children's fears, when they come to us with fears ready-made and built-in, we use these fears as handles to manipulate them and get them to to do what we want. Instead of trying to whittle down their fears, we build them up, often to monstrous size. For we like children who are a little afraid of us, docile, deferential children, though not, of course, if they are so obviously afraid that they threaten our image of ourselves as kind, lovable people whom there is no reason to fear. We find ideal the kind of "good" children who are just enough afraid of us to do everything we want, without making us feel that fear of us is what is making them do it.

We destroy the disinterested (I do *not* mean *un*interested) love of learning in children, which is so strong when they are small, by encouraging and compelling them to work for petty and contemptible rewards—gold stars, or papers marked 100 and tacked to the wall, or A's on report cards, or honor rolls, or dean's lists, or Phi Beta Kappa keys —in short, for the ignoble satisfaction of feeling that they are better than someone else. We encourage them to feel that the end and aim of all they do in school is nothing more than to get a good mark on a test, or to impress someone with what they seem to know. We kill, not only their curiosity, but their feeling that it is a good and admirable thing to be curious, so that by the age of ten most of them will not ask questions, and will show a good deal of scorn for the few who do.

In many ways, we break down children's convictions that things make sense, or their hope that things may prove to make sense. We do it, first of all, by breaking up life into arbitrary and disconnected hunks of subject matter, which we then try to "integrate" by such artificial and irrelevant devices as having children sing Swiss folk songs while they are studying the geography of Switzerland, or do arithmetic problems about rail-splitting while they are studying the boyhood of Lincoln. Furthermore, we continually confront them with what is senseless, ambiguous, and contradictory; worse, we do it without knowing that we are doing it, so that, hearing nonsense shoved at them as if it were sense, they come to feel that the source of their confusion lies not in the material but in their own stupidity. Still further, we cut children off from their own common sense and the world of reality by requiring them to play with and shove around words and symbols that have little or no meaning to them. Thus we turn the vast majority of our students into the kind of people for whom all symbols are meaningless; who cannot use symbols as a way of learning about and dealing with reality; who cannot understand written instructions; who, even if they read books, come out knowing no more than when they went in; who may have a few new words rattling around in their heads, but whose mental models of the world remain unchanged and, indeed, impervious to change. The minority, the able and successful students, we are very likely to turn into something different but just as dangerous: the kind of people who can manipulate words and symbols fluently while keeping themselves largely divorced from the reality for which they stand; the kind of people who like to speak in large generalities but grow silent or indignant if someone asks for an example of what they are talking about; the kind of people who, in their discussions of world affairs, coin and use such words as megadeaths and megacorpses, with scarcely a thought to the blood and suffering these words imply.

We encourage children to act stupidly, not only by scaring and confusing them, but by boring them, by filling up their days with dull, repetitive tasks that make little or no claim on their attention or demands on their intelligence. Our hearts leap for joy at the sight of a roomful of children all slogging away at some imposed task, and we are all the more pleased and satisfied if someone tells us that the children don't really like what they are doing. We tell ourselves that this drudgery, this endless busywork, is good preparation for life, and we fear that without it children would be hard to "control." But why must this busywork be so dull? Why not give tasks that are interesting and demanding? Because, in schools where every task must be completed and every answer must be right, if we give children more demanding tasks they will be fearful and will instantly insist that we show them how to do the job. When you have acres of paper to fill up with pencil marks, you have no time to waste on the luxury of thinking. By such means children are firmly established in the habit of using only a small part of their thinking capacity. They feel that school is a place where they must spend most of their time doing dull tasks in a dull way. Before long they are deeply settled in a rut of unintelligent behavior from which most of them could not escape even if they wanted to.

School tends to be a dishonest as well as a nervous place. We adults are not often honest with children, least of all in school. We tell them, not what we think, but what we feel they ought to think; or what other people feel or tell us they ought to think. Pressure groups find it easy to weed out of our classrooms, texts, and libraries whatever facts, truths, and ideas they happen to find unpleasant or inconvenient. And we are not even as truthful with children as we could safely be, as the parents, politicians, and pressure groups would let us be. Even in the most non-controversial areas our teaching, the books, and the textbooks we give children present a dishonest and distorted picture of the world.

The fact is that we do not feel an obligation to be truthful to children. We are like the managers and manipulators of news in Washington, Moscow, London, Peking, and Paris, and all the other capitals of the world. We think it our right and our duty, not to tell the truth, but to say whatever will best serve our cause—in this case, the cause of

making children grow up into the kind of people
we want them to be, thinking whatever we want
them to think. We have only to convince ourselves
(and we are very easily convinced) that a lie will
be "better" for the children than the truth, and
we will lie. We don't always need even that excuse;
we often lie only for our own convenience.

Worse yet, we are not honest about ourselves,
our own fears, limitations, weaknesses, prejudices,
motives. We present ourselves to children as if we
were gods, all-knowing, all-powerful, always
rational, always just, always right. This is worse
than any lie we could tell about ourselves. I have
more than once shocked teachers by telling them
that when kids ask me a question to which I don't
know the answer, I say, "I haven't the faintest
idea"; or that when I make a mistake, as I often
do, I say, "I goofed again"; or that when I am trying to do something I am no good at, like paint in
water colors or play a clarinet or bugle, I do it
in front of them so they can see me struggling with
it, and can realize that not all adults are good at
everything. If a child asks me to do something that
I don't want to do, I tell him that I won't do it
because I don't want to do it, instead of giving him
a list of "good" reasons sounding as if they had
come down from the Supreme Court. Interestingly
enough, this rather open way of dealing with children works quite well. If you tell a child that you
won't do something because you don't want to, he
is very likely to accept that as a fact which he
cannot change; if you ask him to stop doing something because it drives you crazy, there is a very
good chance that, without further talk, he will
stop, because he knows what that is like.

We are, above all, dishonest about our feelings, and it is this sense of dishonesty of feeling that makes the atmosphere of so many schools so unpleasant. The people who write books that teachers have to read say over and over again that a teacher must love all the children in a class, all of them equally. If by this they mean that a teacher must do the best he can for every child in a class, that he has an equal responsibility for every child's welfare, an equal concern for his problems, they are right. But when they talk of love they don't mean this; they mean feelings, affection, the kind of pleasure and joy that one person can get from the existence and company of another. And this is not something that can be measured out in little spoonfuls, everyone getting the same amount.

In a discussion of this in a class of teachers, I once said that I liked some of the kids in my class much more than others and that, without saying which ones I liked best, I had told them so. After all, this is something that children know, whatever we tell them; it is futile to lie about it. Naturally, these teachers were horrified. "What a terrible thing to say!" one said. "I love all the children in my class exactly the same." Nonsense; a teacher who says this is lying, to herself or to others, and probably doesn't like any of the children very much. Not that there is anything wrong with that; plenty of adults don't like children, and there is no reason why they should. But the trouble is they feel they should, which makes them feel guilty, which makes them feel resentful, which in turn makes them try to work off their guilt with indulgence and their resentment with subtle cruelties—cruelties of a kind that can be seen in many classrooms. Above all, it makes them put on the phony, syrupy, sickening voice and manner, and the fake smiles and forced, bright laughter that children see so much of in school, and rightly resent and hate.

As we are not honest with them, so we won't let children be honest with us. To begin with, we require them to take part in the fiction that school is a wonderful place and that they love every minute of it. They learn early that not to like school or the teacher is *verboten*, not to be said, not even to be thought. I have known a child, otherwise healthy, happy, and wholly delightful, who at the age of five was being made sick with worry by the fact that she did not like her kindergarten teacher. Robert Heinemann worked for a number of years with remedial students whom ordinary schools were hopelessly unable to deal with. He found that what choked up and froze the minds of these children was above all else the fact that they could not express, they could hardly even acknowledge the fear, shame, rage, and hatred that school and their teachers had aroused in them. In a situation in which they were and felt free to express these feelings to themselves and others, they were able once again to begin learning. Why can't we say to children what I used to say to fifth graders who got sore at me, "The law says you have to go to school; it doesn't say you have to like it, and it doesn't say you have to like me either." This might make school more bearable for many children.

Children hear all the time, "Nice people don't say such things." They learn early in life that for unknown reasons they must not talk about a large part of what they think and feel, are most inter-

ested in, and worried about. It is a rare child who,
anywhere in his growing up, meets even one older
person with whom he can talk openly about what
most interests him, concerns him, worries him.
This is what rich people are buying for their
troubled kids when for $25 per hour they send
them to psychiatrists. Here is someone to whom
you can speak honestly about whatever is on your
mind, without having to worry about his getting
mad at you. But do we have to wait until a child
is snowed under by his fears and troubles to give
him this chance? And do we have to take the time
of a highly trained professional to hear what,
earlier in his life, that child might have told any-
body who was willing to listen sympathetically and
honestly? The workers in a project called Street-
corner Research, in Cambridge, Mass., have found
that nothing more than the opportunity to talk
openly and freely about themselves and their lives,
to people who would listen without judging, and
who were interested in them as human beings
rather than as problems to be solved or disposed of,
has totally remade the lives and personalities of a
number of confirmed and seemingly hopeless
juvenile delinquents. Can't we learn something
from this? Can't we clear a space for honesty and
openness and self-awareness in the lives of growing children? Do we have to make them wait
until they are in a jam before giving them a chance
to say what they think?

Behind much of what we do in school lie some
ideas, that could be expressed roughly as follows:
(1) Of the vast body of human knowledge, there
are certain bits and pieces that can be called

essential, that everyone should know; (2) the extent to which a person can be considered educated, qualified to live intelligently in today's world and be a useful member of society, depends on the amount of this essential knowledge that he carries about with him; (3) it is the duty of schools, therefore, to get as much of this essential kowledge as possible into the minds of children. Thus we find ourselves trying to poke certain facts, recipes, and ideas down the gullets of every child in school, whether the morsel interests him or not, even if it frightens him or sickens him, and even if there are other things that he is much more interested in learning.

These ideas are absurd and harmful nonsense. We will not begin to have true education or real learning in our schools until we sweep this nonsense out of the way. Schools should be a place where children learn what they most want to know, instead of what we think they ought to know. The child who wants to know something remembers it and uses it once he has it; the child who learns something to please or appease someone else forgets it when the need for pleasing or the danger of not appeasing is past. This is why children quickly forget all but a small part of what they learn in school. It is of no use or interest to them; they do not want, or expect, or even intend to remember it. The only difference between bad and good students in this respect is that the bad students forget right away, while the good students are careful to wait until after the exam. If for no other reason, we could well afford to throw out most of what we teach in school because the children throw out almost all of it anyway.

The notion of a curriculum, an essential body of knowledge, would be absurd even if children remembered everything we "taught" them. We don't and can't agree on what knowledge is essential. The man who has trained himself in some special field of knowledge or competence thinks, naturally, that his specialty should be in the curriculum. The classical scholars want Greek and Latin taught; the historians shout for more history; the mathematicians urge more math and the scientists more science; the modern language experts want all children taught French, or Spanish, or Russian; and so on. Everyone wants to get his specialty into the act, knowing that as the demand for his special knowledge rises, so will the price that he can charge for it. Who wins this struggle and who loses depends not on the real needs of children or even of society, but on who is most skillful in public relations, who has the best educational lobbyists, who best can capitalize on events that have nothing to do with education, like the appearance of Sputnik in the night skies.

The idea of the curriculum would not be valid even if we could agree what ought to be in it. For knowledge itself changes. Much of what a child learns in school will be found, or thought, before many years, to be untrue. I studied physics at school from a fairly up-to-date text that proclaimed that the fundamental law of physics was the law of conservation of matter—matter is not created or destroyed. I had to scratch that out before I left school. In economics at college I was taught many things that were not true of our economy then, and many more that are not true now. Not for many years after I left college did I learn that the

Greeks, far from being a detached and judicious people surrounded by chaste white temples, were hot-tempered, noisy, quarrelsome, and liked to cover their temples with gold leaf and bright paint; or that most of the citizens of Imperial Rome, far from living in houses in which the rooms surrounded an atrium, or central court, lived in multi-story tenements, one of which was perhaps the largest building in the ancient world. The child who really remembered everything he heard in school would live his life believing many things that were not so.

Moreover, we cannot possibly judge what knowledge will be most needed forty, or twenty, or even ten years from now. At school, I studied Latin and French. Few of the teachers who claimed then that Latin was essential would make as strong a case for it now; and the French might better have been Spanish, or better yet, Russian. Today the schools are busy teaching Russian; but perhaps they should be teaching Chinese, or Hindi, or who-knows-what? Besides physics, I studied chemistry, then perhaps the most popular of all science courses; but I would probably have done better to study biology, or ecology, if such a course had been offered (it wasn't). We always find out, too late, that we don't have the experts we need, that in the past we studied the wrong things; but this is bound to remain so. Since we can't know what knowledge will be most needed in the future, it is senseless to try to teach it in advance. Instead, we should try to turn out people who love learning so much and learn so well that they will be able to learn whatever needs to be learned.

How can we say, in any case, that one piece of

knowledge is more important than another, or indeed, what we really say, that some knowledge is essential and the rest, as far as school is concerned, worthless? A child who wants to learn something that the school can't and doesn't want to teach him will be told not to waste his time. But how can we say that what he wants to know is less important than what we want him to know? We must ask how much of the sum of human knowledge anyone can know at the end of his schooling. Perhaps a millionth. Are we then to believe that one of these millionths is so much more important than another? Or that our social and national problems will be solved if we can just figure out a way to turn children out of schools knowing two millionths of the total, instead of one? Our problems don't arise from the fact that we lack experts enough to tell us what needs to be done, but out of the fact that we do not and will not do what we know needs to be done now.

Learning is not everything, and certainly one piece of learning is as good as another. One of my brightest and boldest fifth graders was deeply interested in snakes. He knew more about snakes than anyone I've ever known. The school did not offer herpetology; snakes were not in the curriculum; but as far as I was concerned, any time he spent learning about snakes was better spent than in ways I could think of to spend it; not least of all because, in the process of learning about snakes, he learned a great deal more about many other things than I was able to "teach" those unfortunates in my class who were not interested in anything at all. In another fifth-grade class, studying Romans in Britain, I saw a boy trying to read a science book behind the cover of his desk. He was spotted, and made to put the book away, and listen to the teacher; with a heavy sigh he did so. What was gained here? She traded a chance for an hour's real learning about science for, at best, an hour's temporary learning about history— much more probably no learning at all, just an hour's worth of daydreaming and resentful thoughts about school.

It is not subject matter that makes some learning more valuable than others, but the spirit in which the work is done. If a child is doing the kind of learning that most children do in school, when they learn at all—swallowing words, to spit back at the teacher on demand—he is wasting his time, or rather, we are wasting it for him. This learning will not be permanent, or relevant, or useful. But a child who is learning naturally, following his curiosity where it leads him, adding to his mental model of reality whatever he needs and can find a place for, and rejecting without fear or guilt what he does not need, is growing—in knowledge, in the love of learning, and in the ability to learn. He is on his way to becoming the kind of person we need in our society, and that our "best" schools and colleges are *not* turning out, the kind of person who, in Whitney Griswold's words, seeks and finds meaning, truth, and enjoyment in everything he does. All his life he will go on learning. Every experience will make his mental model of reality more complete and more true to life, and thus make him more able to deal realistically, imaginatively, and constructively with whatever new experience life throws his way.

We cannot have real learning in school if we

think it is our duty and our right to tell children what they must learn. We cannot know, at any moment, what particular bit of knowledge or understanding a child needs most, will most strengthen and best fit his model of reality. Only he can do this. He may not do it very well, but he can do it a hundred times better than we can. The most we can do is try to help, by letting him know roughly what is available and where he can look for it. Choosing what he wants to learn and what he does not is something he must do for himself.

There is one more reason, and the most important one, why we must reject the idea of school and classroom as places where, most of the time, children are doing what some adult tells them to do. The reason is that there is no way to coerce children without making them afraid, or more afraid. We must not try to fool ourselves into thinking that this is not so. The would-be progressives, who until recently had great influence over most American public school education, did not recognize this —and still do not. They thought, or at least talked and wrote as if they thought, that there were good ways and bad ways to coerce children (the bad ones mean, harsh, cruel, the good ones gentle, persuasive, subtle, kindly), and that if they avoided the bad and stuck to the good they would do no harm. This was one of their greatest mistakes, and the main reason why the revolution they hoped to accomplish never took hold.

The idea of painless, non-threatening coercion is an illusion. Fear is the inseparable companion of coercion, and its inescapable consequence. If you think it your duty to make children do what you want, whether they will or not, then it follows inexorably that you must make them afraid of what will happen to them if they don't do what you want. You can do this in the old-fashioned way, openly and avowedly, with the threat of harsh words, infringement of liberty, or physical punishment. Or you can do it in the modern way, subtly, smoothly, quietly, by withholding the acceptance and approval which you and others have trained the children to depend on; or by making them feel that some retribution awaits them in the future, too vague to imagine but too implacable to escape. You can, as many skilled teachers do, learn to tap with a word, a gesture, a look, even a smile, the great reservoir of fear, shame, and guilt that to-day's children carry around inside them. Or you can simply let your own fears, about what will happen to you if the children don't do what you want, reach out and infect them. Thus the children will feel more and more that life is full of dangers from which only the goodwill of adults like you can protect them, and that this goodwill is perishable and must be earned anew each day.

The alternative—I can see no other—is to have schools and classrooms in which each child in his own way can satisfy his curiosity, develop his abilities and talents, pursue his interests, and from the adults and older children around him get a glimpse of the great variety and richness of life. In short, the school should be a great smörgåsbord of intellectual, artistic, creative, and athletic activities, from which each child could take whatever he wanted, and as much as he wanted, or as little. When Anna was in the sixth grade, the year after she was in my class, I mentioned this idea to her. After describing very sketchily how such a school might be run, and what the children might do, I said, "Tell me, what do you think of it? Do you think it would work? Do you think the kids would learn anything?" She said, with utmost conviction, "Oh, yes, it would be wonderful!" She was silent for a minute or two, perhaps remembering her own generally unhappy schooling. Then she said thoughtfully, "You know, kids really like to learn; we just don't like being pushed around."

No, they don't; and we should be grateful for that. So let's stop pushing them around, and give them a chance.